CW00972697

MICRO

2000 QUICK REFERENCE

Nancy Warner

201 West 103rd Street, Indianapolis, Indiana 46290

MICROSOFT® WORD 2000 QUICK REFERENCE

ISBN: 0-7897-2031-0

International ISBN: 0-7897-2089-2

Library of Congress Catalog Card Number: 99-61237

Printed in the United States of America

First Printing: *June 1999*

01   00   99   4   3   2   1

TRADEMARKS

Executive Editor
Greg Wiegand

Acquisitions Editor
Stephanie McComb

Development Editor
Christy Parrish

Managing Editor
Thomas F. Hayes

Copy Editor
Julie McNamee

Indexer
Sandra Henselmeier

Proofreader
Jeanne Clark

Technical Editor
Bill Bruns

Layout Technician
Steve Geiselman

Book Designer
Louisa Klucznik

ACCEPT OR REJECT CHANGES

When you are ready to finalize tracked changes in a document, you can determine which changes to accept and which to reject.

Quick Tip

Feature	Button	Keyboard Shortcut
Revision Marks Toggle	🗖	Ctrl)+⬥Shift)+E)

Review Revision Marks

1. Right-click the **Revision Marks** 🗖 button on the status bar and choose **Accept or Reject Changes** from the shortcut menu.

2. Click the **Find** ⟶ Find button and Word searches for, finds, and highlights the first (if any) occurrence of a tracked change. Word automatically takes you to the next tracked change after you accept or reject a selected change. If you don't want to accept or reject a particular tracked change, click one of the **Find** buttons to move to the next change.

3. Click the **OK** ok button to continue checking from the beginning of the document (if you started anywhere but the beginning) or to acknowledge that Word found no other changes.

See Also Compare Documents, Track Changes

ACTIVE DOCUMENT
see Workspace   pg 174

ADD-INS

Add-ins are additional programs that you can install to increase the custom commands and features in Word. Add-ins only remain loaded during your current Word session, unless you load them automatically when you start Word.

2

Load an Add-In

1. Choose **Tools, Templates and Add-Ins** to open the Templates and Add-ins dialog box.

2. Click the global templates and add-ins options in the **Checked items are currently loaded** scroll box if your add-in is already added to your global template.

3. Click the **Add** [Add...] button if your add-in is not currently loaded. The Add Template dialog box will automatically open to the Templates folder. This is where you should place any add-ins you want to load.

4. Double-click to select the file and return to the Templates and Add-ins dialog box.

5. Click the **OK** [OK] button to accept your changes.

Automatically Start an Add-In

1. Choose **Tools, Options; File Locations** tab to note the location of your Startup folder.

2. Open an Explorer window and place the add-in you want to automatically load, in the Word Startup folder. The next time you start Word, the add-in will load automatically.

Unload an Add-In

1. Choose **Tools, Templates and Add-Ins** to open the Templates and Add-ins dialog box.

2. Click to deselect the global templates and add-ins options in the **Checked items are currently loaded** scroll box if your add-in is already added to your global template.

3. Click the **OK** [OK] button to accept your changes.

Delete an Add-In

1. Choose **Tools, Templates and Add-Ins** to open the Templates and Add-ins dialog box.

2. Click the global templates and add-ins options in the **Checked items are currently loaded** scroll box if your add-in is already added to your global template.

3. Click the **Remove** [Remove] button whether your add-in is currently loaded or not.

4. Click the **OK** [OK] button to accept your changes.

See Also Templates

ALIGNMENT

When you enter text into a document, the text will automatically align flush (even) with the left margin. However, you can change the alignment of text at any time, before or after you have entered the text.

Quick Tips

Feature	Button	Keyboard Shortcut
Align Left	☰	Ctrl+L
Center	☰	Ctrl+E
Align Right	☰	Ctrl+R
Justify	☰	Ctrl+J

Click and Type

1. Choose **View**, **Print Layout**.

2. Double-click directly in the document where you want the text to begin and start typing.

Align New Text

1. Click the appropriate alignment button on the Formatting toolbar and begin typing.

Align Existing Text

1. Select the text you want to align. Or, place the cursor somewhere in the paragraph you want to align.

2. Click the **Align Right** ☰ button on the Formatting toolbar to align right; the **Center** ☰ button to center text; the **Align Left** ☰ button to align left, or the

Justify 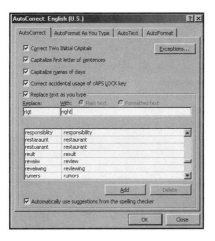 button to justify (make flush with both margins) your text.

See Also Indenting, Page Setup

ANIMATIONS
see Text Effects   pg 158

AUTOCORRECT

Word 2000 lets you automatically correct yourself if you consistently make the same typing errors in your documents. The most common errors to automatically correct are capitalization options, spelling checker corrections, and AutoCorrect entries.

Replace Text As You Type

1. Choose **Tools, AutoCorrect; AutoCorrect** tab. Click the **Replace text as you type** check box.

2. Type the text you commonly spell wrong in the **Replace** text box. Type the correct text in the **With** text box.

3. Click the **Add** [Add] button to add an automatic correction.

4. Click the **OK** [OK] button to accept your changes.

Delete a Replace Text as You Type Option

1. Choose **Tools**, **AutoCorrect**; **AutoCorrect** tab.

2. Scroll through and click the **Replace text as you type** option that you want to delete.

3. Click the **Delete** [Delete] button and click the **OK** [OK] button to accept your changes.

Deselecting AutoCorrect Options

1. Choose **Tools**, **AutoCorrect**; **AutoCorrect** tab.

2. Click to deselect each AutoCorrect option you don't want to use:

   - **Correct TWo INitial CApitals**

   - **Capitalize first letter of sentences**

   - **Capitalize names of days**

   - **Correct accidental usage of cAPS LOCK key**

   - **Replace text as you type**

   - **Automatically use suggestions from the spelling checker**

3. Click the **OK** [OK] button to accept your changes.

See Also AutoFormat, AutoText, Spelling and Grammar, Symbols

AUTOFIT

You can quickly create tables in Word. Now it is even easier to format the size and spacing of your rows and columns either before or after you have entered your table content.

AutoFit a Table

1. Select the table that you want to automatically fit to its contents.

2. Choose **Table**, **AutoFit** and select any of the following options:

   - **AutoFit to Contents**—sizes the table to fit the content in your table.

- **AutoFit to Window**—spaces the rows and columns so they are symmetrical with the table on the page.

- **Fixed Column Width**—sets the column widths so that they will not increase or decrease with the content entered.

- **Distribute Rows Evenly**—sets the rows to the same height.

- **Distribute Columns Evenly**—sets the columns to the same width.

See Also AutoFormat, Draw Table, Tables

AUTOFORMAT

Microsoft Word helps you format text and tables quickly with an autoformat feature. With AutoFormat you can save valuable time by having Word automatically apply standard styles and formats to your text. You can have Word apply preset colors, fonts, and formats to your tables to give them a professional look in a fraction of the time.

Quick Tips		
Feature	*Button*	*Keyboard Shortcut*
AutoFormat Text		Ctrl + Alt + K
Update AutoFormat		Ctrl + Alt + U
Table AutoFormat	📇	

AutoFormat Text

1. Open the document you want to AutoFormat.

2. Choose **Format, AutoFormat** and click the **Options** Options... button on the AutoFormat dialog box.

3. Select the different options available on the **AutoFormat** tab of the AutoCorrect dialog box.

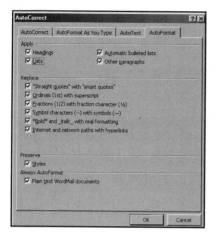

4. Click the OK ⬚ᴏᴋ button on the **AutoFormat** tab to accept changes.

5. Click the OK ⬚ᴏᴋ button on the AutoFormat dialog box to return to the document.

AutoFormat Tables

1. Select the table you want to format.

2. Choose **Table**, **Table AutoFormat** and select one of the available formats in the Table AutoFormat dialog box.

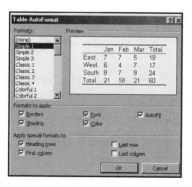

3. Click the OK ⬚ᴏᴋ button to accept changes.

See Also AutoCorrect, AutoText, Fonts, Text, Tables

TIP

Even after you have selected a table AutoFormat, you can determine different formats to apply to the selected table. Selecting and deselecting **Formats to apply** and **Apply special formats to** options will alter your table formats even more.

AUTOSHAPES

Word provides shapes that can be automatically inserted into documents so that you don't have to create them from scratch. This is convenient when you want to use designed shapes in a report or newsletter.

Insert AutoShapes

1. Click the **Drawing** 🔲 button on the Formatting toolbar to open the Drawing toolbar at the bottom of the document.
2. Click the **AutoShapes** [AutoShapes ▾] button and select the particular shape you want to add to your document from the submenu.
3. Click in the document and drag the cross-hatch pointer to the desired shape size.

Change AutoShapes

1. Click the **Drawing** 🔲 button on the Formatting toolbar to open the Drawing toolbar at the bottom of the document.
2. Click directly on the AutoShape you entered in your document.
3. Click **Draw, Change AutoShape** on the Drawing toolbar and select a different shape.

9

Format AutoShapes

1. Right-click the AutoShape you entered in your document and choose **Format AutoShape** from the shortcut menu.

2. Select the following tabs to choose options for formatting your AutoShape:

   - **Colors and Lines**—change the color that fills in the AutoShape and display particular types of lines around the AutoShape.

   - **Size**—size and rotate the AutoShape as well as alter the scale.

   - **Layout**—alter the wrapping style of the AutoShape (how text is flowed around or over the object) and the alignment of the AutoShape in the document.

   - **Web**—type the text you want to display while a Web browser is loading the AutoShape.

3. Click the **OK** button on any of the tabs to accept changes and return to the document.

> **TIP**
> Click the **Drawing** 🎨 button on the Formatting toolbar to toggle between displaying and hiding the Drawing toolbar.

See Also Clip Art, Drawing Tools, WordArt

AUTOSUMMARIZE

This feature summarizes the main points in a document by analyzing sentences that contain frequently used words. These words determine which sentences make up the key points in your document. This is a convenient feature when you have a long document that you need to trim down for a particular reader or report, but want to keep the main points.

Create a Document Summary

1. Choose **Tools, AutoSummarize** to open the AutoSummarize dialog box.

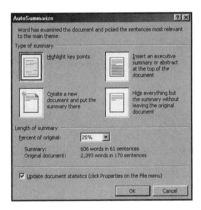

2. Select the **Type of summary** from the four choices available and the **Length of summary** from the **Percentage of original** drop-down list.
3. Click the **OK** ok button. Word automatically highlights the important summary points and opens the AutoSummarize toolbar.

4. Click the **Highlight/Show Only Summary** button to toggle between showing only the information in the summary and the original text.

5. Click the **Percent of Original** scroll arrows to increase or decrease the amount of original document that displays.

6. Click the **Close** button to cancel the summary.

See Also Word Count

AUTOTEXT

AutoText allows you to save commonly used words or phrases as fields that you can add to your documents. You can insert the default AutoText that Word provides or create your own.

Quick Tips	
Feature	*Keyboard Shortcut*
Complete AutoText Entry	F3 or Alt+Ctrl+V
Create AutoText Entry	Alt+F3

Work with AutoText Entries

1. Choose **Insert, AutoText, AutoText** to open the **AutoText** tab of the AutoCorrect dialog box.

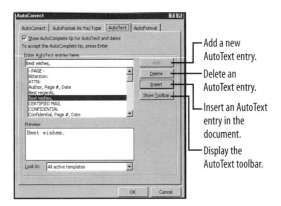

- Add a new AutoText entry.
- Delete an AutoText entry.
- Insert an AutoText entry in the document.
- Display the AutoText toolbar.

2. Type the AutoText entry in the **Enter AutoText entries here** text box.

3. Click the **Add** button to add the AutoText entry.

4. Click the **OK** button to accept the changes and return to the document.

5. Choose **Insert, AutoText, Normal** and click the AutoText entry you want added to your document. The other submenus allow you to use AutoText entries that Word provides.

Turn AutoText Entries Off

1. Choose **Insert, AutoText, AutoText** to open the **AutoText** tab of the AutoCorrect dialog box.

2. Uncheck the **Show AutoComplete tip for AutoText and dates** option.

3. Click the **OK** button to accept the changes and return to the document.

Enter AutoText in a Document

1. Type the first portion of an AutoText entry in your document.

2. Press either the F3 key or Alt+Ctrl+V to automatically complete the entry.

Delete AutoText Entries

1. Choose **Insert**, **AutoText**, **AutoText** to open the **AutoText** tab of the AutoCorrect dialog box.

2. Select the entry in the **AutoText** tab of the AutoCorrect dialog box and choose the **Delete** button.

See Also AutoCorrect, Header and Footer

BACKGROUND

When creating Web pages or desktop publishing documents in Word, you can apply a background to your documents to add visual interest. You can add solid colors as well as fill effects like gradients, textures, patterns, and pictures.

Apply a Document Background Color or Fill Effect

1. Choose **Format**, **Background**, and select the color you want to apply or select the **Fill Effects** command to open the Fill Effects dialog box.

Select a specific color.

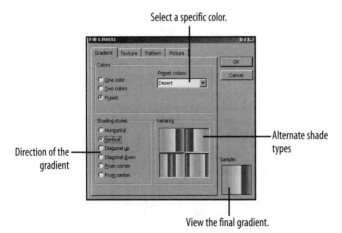

Direction of the gradient

Alternate shade types

View the final gradient.

2. Choose between the **Gradient**, **Texture**, **Pattern**, and **Picture** tabs to apply different effects in the Fill Effects dialog box. The **Sample** window in the bottom-right corner of the dialog box shows you what your background will look like.

3. Click the **OK**  button to accept changes and return to the document.

> **TIP**
>
> Choose **File, Web Page Preview** to see how the document appears with the selected background.

See Also Frames, Shading, Themes, Web pages

BOLD
see Text   pg 155

BOOKMARKS

Word allows you to create bookmarks that you can use to mark text, graphics, or other elements for cross reference in a document.

Insert a Bookmark

1. Select the text or object where you want to add a bookmark.

2. Choose **Insert, Bookmark** to open the Bookmark dialog box.

3. Type in a **Bookmark name** and click the **Add** button.

4. Repeat steps 1–3 for each bookmark you want to insert.

5. Click the **Cancel** button when you want to return to the document.

Delete a Bookmark

1. Choose **Insert**, **Bookmark** to open the Bookmark dialog box.

2. Select the **Bookmark name** and click the **Delete** [Delete] button.

3. Repeat steps 1–2 for each bookmark you want to delete.

4. Click the **Cancel** [Cancel] button when you want to return to the document.

Go To a Bookmark

1. Choose **Insert**, **Bookmark** to open the Bookmark dialog box.

2. Select the **Bookmark name** and click the **Go To** [Go To] button.

3. Repeat steps 1–2 for each bookmark you want to go to.

4. Click the **Cancel** [Cancel] button when you want to return to the document.

See Also Comments, Cross-References, Fields, Index

BORDERS

You can add a border to any or all sides of a paragraph, selected text, document, or object.

Add Text Borders

1. Select the text or place the cursor in your document where you want to add a border.

2. Click the **Borders** ⊞ button on the Formatting toolbar and select the type of border you want to apply to the document from the drop-down list.

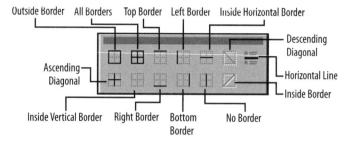

Outside Border   All Borders   Top Border   Left Border   Inside Horizontal Border
Descending Diagonal
Ascending Diagonal
Horizontal Line
Inside Border
Inside Vertical Border   Right Border   Bottom Border   No Border

Format Borders

1. Place the cursor in the paragraph that contains a border.

2. Choose **Format, Borders and Shading; Borders** tab.

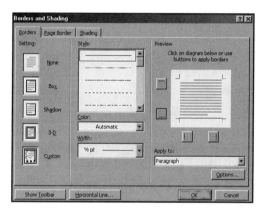

3. Select from the **Setting, Style, Color,** and **Width** options.

4. Click the **Preview** diagram to apply borders to particular sides of the selected paragraph.

5. Click the **OK** ![OK] button to accept changes and return to the document.

Add Page Borders

1. Choose **Format, Borders and Shading; Page Border** tab.

2. Select from the **Setting, Style, Color,** and **Width** options.

3. Click the **Preview** diagram to apply borders to the document.

4. Click the **Apply to** drop-down list and select from the page border options.

5. Click the **OK** [OK] button to accept changes and return to the document.

Add Graphic Borders

1. Select the graphic to which you want to add a border.

2. Choose **Format, Borders and Shading; Borders** tab.

3. Select the type of border **Setting, Style** of the line, **Color** of the line, and the **Width** of the line.

4. Click the **OK** [OK] button to accept changes and return to the document.

TIP

If in the Borders dialog box, you can click on the different borders in the **Preview** area to place a border line on a particular side of the graphic.

Alter Table Borders

1. Place the cursor in the table that contains a border.

2. Choose **Format, Borders and Shading; Borders** tab.

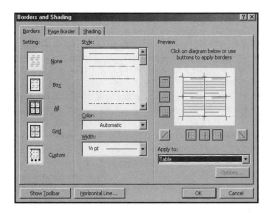

3. Select from the **Setting, Style, Color,** and **Width** options.

4. Click the **Preview** diagram to alter the borders on particular sides of the selected table.

5. Click the OK button to accept changes and return to the document.

View Tables and Borders Toolbar

1. Choose **View, Toolbars, Tables and Borders** to open the Tables and Borders toolbar.

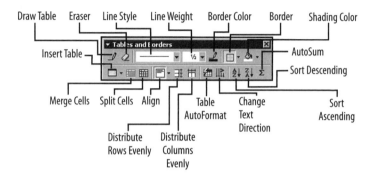

2. Click the **Close** ⊠ button to close the toolbar.

See Also Columns, Shading, Tables

BREAKS

When a page is filled with text, Word automatically begins a new page by inserting a page break for you; however, there are times when you want to manually insert a page or section break. Perhaps you want to have a section of multiple columns in the middle of a one-column page.

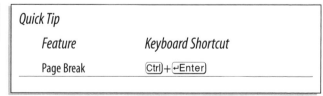

Quick Tip	
Feature	*Keyboard Shortcut*
Page Break	Ctrl+⏎Enter

Create a Break

1. Choose **Insert, Break** to open the Break dialog box.

Page break at the point of the cursor.

Column break at the point of the cursor.

Line break at the point of the cursor.

Start a new section at the top of the next page.

Insert a section break without inserting a page break.

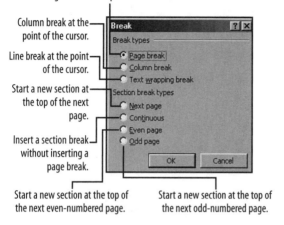

Start a new section at the top of the next even-numbered page.

Start a new section at the top of the next odd-numbered page.

2. Select the type of page break you want to insert in your document.

3. Click the **OK** [OK] button to accept changes and return to the document.

Delete a Break

1. Place the cursor at the beginning of the break.

2. Press the Del key.

See Also Columns, Pagination

BROWSE

The Select Browse Object menu allows you to click on items you want to use to browse through an active document.

Use the Select Browse Object Menu

1. Click the **Select Browse Object** button.

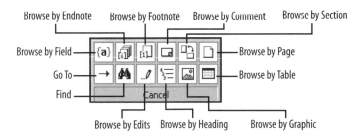

Browse by Endnote   Browse by Footnote   Browse by Comment   Browse by Section

Browse by Field

Go To

Find

Browse by Page

Browse by Table

Browse by Edits   Browse by Heading   Browse by Graphic

2. Click on the item you want to browse by. Word automatically takes you to the next item you selected.

See Also Find, Workspace

BULLETED LISTS

Bulleted lists are useful for presenting a series of items when alpha or numeric order doesn't matter.

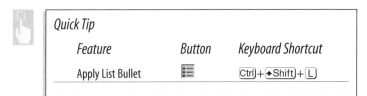

Quick Tip

Feature	Button	Keyboard Shortcut
Apply List Bullet		Ctrl + ⬆Shift + L

Bullet New Text

1. Click the **Bullets** button on the Formatting toolbar and begin typing.
2. Click the **Bullets** button again when you have finished your list.

Bullet Existing Text

1. Select the text you want to bullet.
2. Click the **Bullets** button on the Formatting toolbar. Notice that a bullet is added to each paragraph, not each sentence.

Alter Bullets

1. Select the text containing the bullets you want to alter.
2. Choose **Format, Bullets and Numbering; Bulleted** tab.

3. Double-click the style of bullets you want to display.

Customize Bullets

1. Select the text containing the bullets you want to alter.
2. Choose **Format, Bullets and Numbering; Bulleted** tab.
3. Click the **Customize** Customize... button to customize the bullet character.
4. Click the **Font** Font... button to alter the font of the bullet; click the **Bullet** Bullet... button to alter the symbol of the bullet.
5. Click the **OK** OK button to accept changes and return to the document.

Picture Bullets

1. Select the text containing the bullets you want to alter.
2. Choose **Format, Bullets and Numbering; Bulleted** tab.
3. Click the **Picture** Picture... button to insert a picture or motion clip for the bullet.
4. Click the **OK** OK button to accept changes and return to the document.

See Also Numbered Lists

CASE CHANGE

Word allows you to easily change the case of text after it is written.

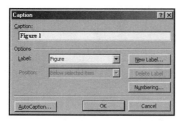

3. Type any additional information you want in the **Caption** text box.

4. Click the **Position** drop-down arrow to select the location of the caption in relation to the object.

5. Click the **OK** [OK] button to return to the document.

TIP

To number your captions, click the **Numbering** [Numbering...] button on the Caption dialog box and select from the **Format** drop-down list options. Click the **OK** [OK] button in both dialog boxes to return to the document.

See Also Drawing Tools, Graphs, Tables

CENTER
see Alignment   pg 3

CHARACTER SPACING

The space above, below, before, and after characters can all be altered. This is convenient when you need a word or group of words to fit into a particular area.

Alter Character Spacing

1. Select the text where you want to alter the character spacing (or the entire document with Ctrl+A).

2. Choose **Format, Font; Character Spacing** tab.

Stretch or compress the
text as a percentage of its
current size horizontally.

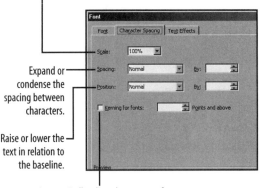

Expand or
condense the
spacing between
characters.

Raise or lower the
text in relation to
the baseline.

Automatically adjust the amount of
space between character combinations.

3. Select from the various character spacing options.
4. Click the **OK** ![OK] button to accept changes and
   return to the document.

See Also Fonts, Line Spacing, Paragraph Spacing, Symbols,
Text

CHARTS

Word allows you to create and add charts to your documents without inserting an Excel worksheet. For more
detailed information on Excel worksheets, see the section
specifically on **Excel Worksheets**.

Insert Chart

1. Choose **Insert, Picture, Chart** to open a generic Excel
   datasheet and default 3D column chart.
2. Type the desired data into the datasheet and the chart
   updates automatically.

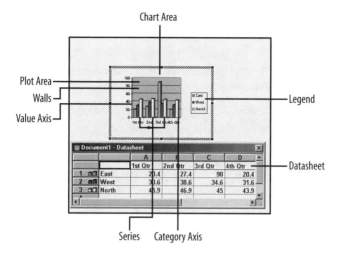

Chart Area

Plot Area
Walls
Value Axis

Legend

Datasheet

Series   Category Axis

3. Click directly in the document to hide the datasheet.

Change the Chart Type

1. Double-click the chart to open it for editing.

2. Right-click one of the value bars in the chart plot area and choose **Chart Type** from the shortcut menu.

3. Select an alternate **Chart type** and **Chart sub-type** in the Chart Type dialog box.

4. Click the **OK** [___OK___] button. The updated chart type appears in the chart.

Alter Chart Options

1. Double-click the chart to open it for editing.

2. Right-click the plot area and choose **Chart Options** from the shortcut menu to open the Chart Options dialog box. Any changes you make to this dialog box automatically appear in the chart preview window on the dialog box.

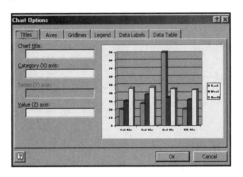

3. Click the following tabs to alter options on your chart:
   - **Titles**—alter the **Chart title** and different axis options.
   - **Axes**—alter the **Primary axis** on your chart.
   - **Gridlines**—add **Category (X) axis Major gridlines** to your chart.
   - **Legend**—alter the **Placement** of the legend in your chart.
   - **Data Labels**—alter the **Data labels** to be more or less descriptive.
   - **Data Table**—select to **Show data table** with your chart.

4. Click the **OK** ▭ OK ▭ button to accept all your chart options and see how your chart has changed.

> **TIP**
>
> To change the pattern and scale of the gridlines, double-click the gridline itself. Then use the Format Gridlines dialog box to make your selections and click the **OK** ▭ OK ▭ button.

Format the Plot Area

1. Double-click the chart to open it for editing.

2. Right-click the plot area and choose **Format Plot Area** from the shortcut menu.

3. Select the **Area** color, **Fill Effects,** and **Border** on the **Patterns** tab of the Format Plot Area dialog box.

4. Click the **OK**  `OK` button to accept your changes and return to the chart.

Format the Chart Area

1. Double-click the chart to open it for editing.

2. Right-click the chart area and choose **Format Chart Area** from the shortcut menu.

3. Click the **Font** tab of the Format Plot Area dialog box. Select the **Font** options you prefer.

4. Click the **Patterns** tab and select a type of **Border** around the chart and any color you want for the chart **Area** itself.

5. Click the **OK** `OK` button to accept your changes and return to the chart.

Format the Axis Scale

1. Double-click the chart to open it for editing.

2. Right-click the Value Axis and choose **Format Axis** from the shortcut menu.

3. Click the **Scale** tab of the Format Axis dialog box.

4. Type different units for the following values (the Auto values are determined by Microsoft Graph):

   ■ **Minimum**—displays the lowest value from all data series.

- **Maximum**—displays the highest value from all data series.

- **Major unit**—choose the major tick mark and gridline intervals.

- **Minor unit**—choose the minor tick mark and gridline intervals.

- **Floor (XY plane) Crosses at**—select where to cross the value and category axis.

5. Click the **OK** [OK] button to accept your changes and return to the chart.

Alter the Datasheet Data

1. Double-click the chart to open it for editing.

2. Click the cell(s) in the datasheet that you want to alter or need to update.

3. Type in the new data and press the (↵Enter) key.

4. Click back in the document to accept your changes.

Edit a Chart in Microsoft Graph

1. Right-click the chart and select **Chart Object, Open** from the shortcut menu.

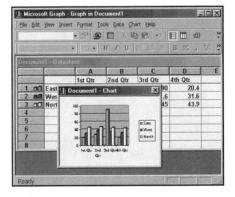

2. Click the cell(s) in the Microsoft Graph that you want to alter or need to update.

3. Choose **File, Update** to save the changes or **File, Exit & Return to Document**.

See Also Excel Worksheets

CLIP ART

Clip art adds visual interest to your Word documents. You
can choose from numerous types of prepared images.

Insert Clip Art

1. Choose **Insert, Picture, Clip Art** to open the Insert
   ClipArt dialog box.

2. Click on the **Categories** of clip art in the **Pictures** tab
   and scroll through the options.

3. Click on the piece of clip art and choose **Insert Clip**
   from the pop-up menu, which inserts the clip art
   into your document.

4. Click the **Close** button to close the Insert ClipArt
   dialog box.

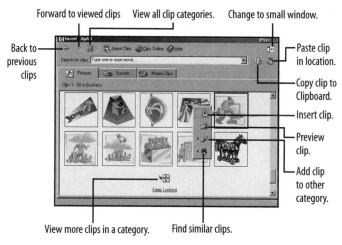

Forward to viewed clips   View all clip categories.   Change to small window.

Back to previous clips

Paste clip in location.

Copy clip to Clipboard.

Insert clip.

Preview clip.

Add clip to other category.

View more clips in a category.   Find similar clips.

Format Clip Art

1. Right-click the clip art you entered in your document
   and choose **Format Picture** from the shortcut menu.

2. Select the following tabs to choose options for formatting your clip art:

   ■ **Colors and Lines**—Change the color that fills in the
     clip art.

   ■ **Size**—Size and rotate the clip art as well as alter the
     scale.

- **Layout** —Alter the wrapping style of the clip art (how text is flowed around or over the object) and the alignment of the clip art in the document.

- **Picture**—Set the crop size of the object and control the color, brightness, and object contrast.

- **Web**—Alter the text displayed when this graphic is loading on a Web page.

3. Click the **OK** [OK] button sto accept changes and return to the document.

See Also Borders

CLIPBOARD
see Copy and Cut   pg 34

CLOSE

When you finish working on a document, you can close it and continue to work on other documents. You can close a file with or without saving changes.

Quick Tip		
Feature	*Button*	*Keyboard Shortcut*
Close Document	📱	Alt+F4 or
		Ctrl+F4 or
		Ctrl+W

Close a Document

1. Click the **Close** ☒ button. If you made changes to the document, Word asks whether you want to save the changes.

2. Click the **Yes** [Yes] button to save changes and close the document; click the **No** [No] button to close the document without saving changes; click the **Cancel**

[Cancel] button to return to working in your document
without closing it or saving any changes.

See Also Save Documents

COLOR
see Shading   pg 130

COLUMNS

You can display text in multiple columns on a page in a
Word document. This is convenient when you want to create a brochure or newsletter or even differentiate between
sections of a document.

Create New Columns

1. Click the **Columns** button on the Standard toolbar
   and select the number of columns you want.
2. Begin typing your text. Your text will appear in columns
   until you insert a break.

Create Columns from Existing Text

1. Select the text you want to convert to columns.
2. Click the **Columns** button on the Standard toolbar
   and select the number of columns you want.

TIP

A column break must be added to move to the next column
when entering text. See Breaks for more information.

Format Columns

1. Select the columnar text you want to format.
2. Choose **Format**, **Columns** to open the Columns dialog
   box.

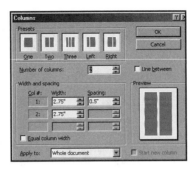

3. Select the column **Presets** options or the **Number of columns** from the spin box control. You can also manually alter the column **Width** and **Spacing** options and insert a graphic line between the columns.

4. Click the **OK** button to accept changes and return to your document.

See Also Breaks, Tables

COMMENTS

When working in a document, you might find that you need to add a note in your document reminding yourself to check on something or verify some information when you work on the document later. Or, perhaps you are sharing documents with other users and want to keep track of the comments that each user makes.

Quick Tip		
Feature	*Button*	*Keyboard Shortcut*
Comment	🔲	Ctrl+Alt+M

Insert Comments

1. Select the text you want to comment on or place the cursor at the location where you want to insert a comment.

2. Choose **Insert, Comment** to open the Comment window.

3. Type your comment and click the **Close** [Close] button when finished. The text that has been commented on will be highlighted and contain a comment number.

TIP

Move the mouse pointer over the highlighted comment indicator and the comment appears in a ScreenTip.

View All Comments

1. Choose **View, Comments** to open the Comments window.
2. Click the **Close** [Close] button when finished viewing.

Edit Comments

1. Select the highlighted text, right-click and choose **Edit Comment** from the shortcut menu.
2. Type the changes into the comment area and click the **Close** [Close] button to return to the document.

Delete Comments

1. Select the highlighted text, right-click, and choose **Delete Comment** from the shortcut menu.

See Also Protect Documents, Share Documents, Track Changes

COMPARE DOCUMENTS

A quick way to find the differences between two documents is to use the **Compare Documents** tool.

Compare Two Documents

1. Open the document in which you want the comparison made; this will be the *current document*.
2. Choose **Tools, Track Changes, Compare Documents**.
3. Locate the **File name** of the *original* file you want to compare with the current document.

4. Click the **Open** button and any old text appears in a different color with strikethrough; any new text appears in another color.

See Also Accept or Reject Changes, Merge Documents, Track Changes, Versions

COPY AND CUT

You can share information within and between documents in Word (and other Office applications) by copying and cutting text and objects. You can now copy and cut up to 12 different items onto the Clipboard at a time. The Clipboard is where items are stored before you paste them.

Quick Tips		
Feature	*Button*	*Keyboard Shortcut*
Copy	📋	Ctrl+C or Ctrl+Insert
Copy Format	🖌	Ctrl+◆Shift+C
Copy Text Only		◆Shift+F2
Cut	✂	Ctrl+X or ◆Shift+Del

Copy

1. Select the text or object you want to copy.
2. Click the **Copy** 📋 button on the Standard toolbar. The original text remains in this location and a copy is placed on the Clipboard ready to be pasted.

Cut

1. Select the text or object you want to cut.
2. Click the **Cut** ✂ button on the Standard toolbar. This removes the text from its location and places it on the Clipboard ready to be pasted.

Copy Multiple Items

1. Choose **View, Toolbars, Clipboard** to open the new Clipboard toolbar.
2. Select an item you want to copy and then click the **Copy** 📋 button on the Clipboard toolbar. Repeat this process each time you select an item (up to 12 items). You can also use the original **Copy** 📋 and **Cut** ✂ buttons on the Standard toolbar to place items on the Clipboard toolbar.

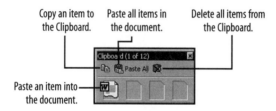

Copy an item to the Clipboard. Paste all items in the document. Delete all items from the Clipboard.

Paste an item into the document.

3. Move the mouse pointer over the items on the Clipboard toolbar and a ScreenTip displays what is contained in each copied clip (unless the clip is extensive, then only part of it will display).
4. Move the mouse pointer to where you want to insert the text or object. Click the clip to paste the item in the document.

TIP

The Clipboard toolbar automatically appears when you click the **Cut** ✂ or **Copy** 🖹 button multiple times. Click the **Close** ✖ button to close the Clipboard toolbar, or choose **View, Toolbars, Clipboard** to toggle the toolbar closed.

See Also Format Painter, Move Text, Objects, Paste

CROSS-REFERENCES

Word allows you to create a cross-reference in a document to an item in a different location in the same document. You can create references to styles, bookmarks, captions, or numbered paragraphs.

Insert a Cross-Reference

1. Type the introductory text that begins the cross-reference.

2. Choose **Insert, Cross-reference** to open the Cross-reference dialog box.

3. Click the **Reference type** drop-down list and select the type of item you want to refer to.

4. Click the **Insert reference to** drop-down list and select the information you want inserted in the document.

5. Click the **For which heading** option for the item you want to refer to.

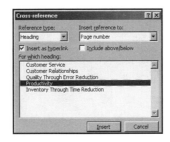

6. Click the **Insert** [Insert] button and the **Close** [Close]
   button to return to the document.

TIP

You can link to a cross-reference by selecting the **Insert as hyperlink** option in the Cross-reference dialog box.

Modify a Cross-Reference

1. Select only the cross-reference visible in the main document.

2. Choose **Insert, Cross-reference** to open the Cross-reference dialog box.

3. Click the **Insert reference to** drop-down list to change the item you want to refer to.

4. Click the **Insert** [Insert] button and the **Close** [Close]
   button to return to the document.

TIP

You can edit the document text that is the cross-reference introductory text at any time.

See Also Bookmarks, Comments, Fields, Index, Table of Contents

DATE AND TIME

Instead of typing the date and time into documents, you can paste a date field in one of several formats that Word makes available.

> ## Quick Tips
>
> | Feature | Keyboard Shortcut |
> |---------|-------------------|
> | Date Field | Alt + ⬆Shift + D |
> | Time Field | Alt + ⬆Shift + T |
> | Update Fields | Alt + ⬆Shift + U |

Insert the Date and Time

1. Choose **Insert**, **Date and Time** to open the Date and Time dialog box.

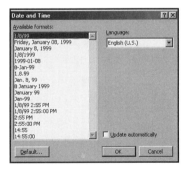

2. Select from the **Available formats** and click the **OK** [OK] button to enter the information into your document as a field.

TIP

Click the **Update automatically** option on the Date and Time dialog box and the format you select automatically becomes a field that updates when you print or open the document. In addition, you can immediately update the field if you right-click on the field and select Update Field.

See Also AutoText

DETECT AND REPAIR

Detect and Repair automatically finds and fixes errors in
your current session of Word. When doing this, have your
installation disks nearby and close any other applications
you have open.

Run Detect and Repair

1. Choose **Help, Detect and Repair** in Word.

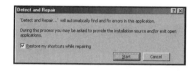

D
E
F

2. Click the **Start** ⎡Start⎤ button in the Detect and
Repair dialog box. Note that the **Restore my shortcuts
while repairing** check box will add the program shortcuts to the Windows Start menu, if selected.

3. Select the other application(s) you are running and
want to **Cancel, Retry,** or **Ignore.**

See Also Help, Office Assistant, Office on the Web

DIALOG BOXES

Windows uses dialog boxes to display information to and
request input from the end user. The different ways you can
provide input are through buttons, text boxes, option buttons (also known as radio buttons), check boxes, spin
boxes, list boxes, and drop-down list boxes.

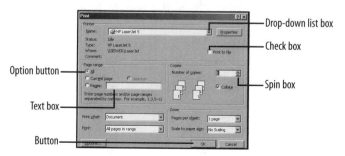

Get Help in a Dialog Box

1. Click the **Help** ⁇ button in the upper-right area of the dialog box title bar.

2. Click the item you need help with and a ScreenTip appears with descriptive information.

3. Click anywhere on your desktop or press the (Esc) key to continue.

Close a Dialog Box

1. Click the **Close** ⌧ button in the upper-right corner on the dialog box title bar or press the (Esc) key. If it happens to be a dialog box where you can *Apply* changes and still must exit the dialog box, you can also click a **Cancel** [Cancel] or **Close** [Close] button to close.

See Also Menus

DOCKED TOOLBAR
see Toolbars   pg 161

DOCUMENT MAP

Word automatically creates a document map when you use built-in heading styles (Heading 1 through Heading 9) and outline-level paragraphs (Level 1 through Level 9).

Use the Document Map

1. Click the **Document Map** ⁇ button to toggle between displaying the document map and your current document view.

2. Click a listed header in the document map to immediately view the document section associated with the header.

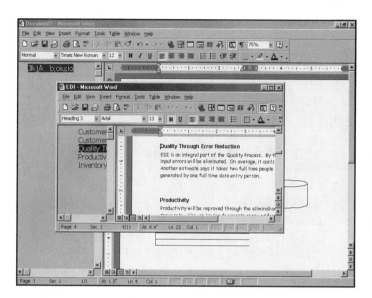

See Also Styles, Views

DRAG AND DROP
see Move Text pg 100

DRAWING TOOLS

Word provides many tools for you to draw and format shapes in your document. Shapes can add interest, information, and references in your documents.

Draw Shapes

1. Click the **Drawing** button on the Standard toolbar to open the Drawing toolbar.

2. Select the shape you want to draw in your document: **Line**, **Arrow**, **Rectangle**, or **Oval**.

3. Click in the document and drag the cross-hatch pointer to the desired shape size.

Add Shape Color

1. Click the shape you want to color in your document.

2. Click the appropriate button on the Drawing toolbar to select how you want to apply the color: **Fill Color** 🖱 and **Line Color** 🖊. Click the desired color.

Alter Shape Style

1. Click on the shape to which you want to apply a style in your document.

2. Click the appropriate button on the Drawing toolbar to select how you want to apply the style: **Line Style** ▤, **Dash Style** ▦, **Arrow Style** 🗏, **Shadow** ▣, and **3-D** ▨.

Rotate Shapes

1. Click the shape you want to rotate in your document.

2. Click the **Free Rotate** 🔄 button on the Drawing toolbar.

3. Click the rotate pointer on one of the object's *round* rotate handles and drag the object to the desired rotation.

See Also AutoShapes, Clip Art, Objects, Text Box, WordArt

DROP CAP

Word allows you to format text so that it uses a large initial capital letter. This is common in articles and newsletters.

Position a Drop Cap

1. Select the text to which you want to apply a drop cap.

2. Choose **Format**, **Drop Cap** to open the Drop Cap dialog box.

3. Click one of the **Position** options.

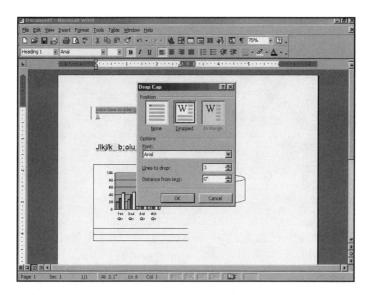

4. Select a **Font** from the drop-down list box for the initial drop cap.

5. Select the **Lines to drop** and the **Distance from text** from each spin box control.

6. Click the **OK** <u>OK</u> button to accept changes and return to the document.

See Also Case Change, Character Spacing, Fonts, Text

EMAIL

You can send the contents of a Word document as the substance of the email message or as an attachment to the email message.

Send a Document as an Email

1. Click the **Email** 🖃 button on the Standard toolbar.

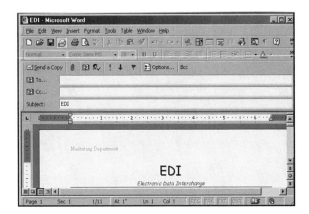

2. Type the **To**, **Cc**, and any changes to the **Subject** line (this defaults to the filename) and any other changes in the document.

3. Click the **Send a Copy** button and it will be sent.

TIP

Click the **Email** 🖼 button in the email document window if you decide not to send the document as an email and want to return to the document.

Send a Document as an Email Attachment

1. Choose **File, Send To, Mail recipient (as Attachment)**. This will open an email message and insert the current document as an attachment.

2. Type the **To, Cc**, any changes to the **Subject** line (this defaults to the filename), and any other changes in the document.

3. Click the **Send** button and it is sent.

See Also Web Pages

EMBEDDED OBJECTS

see Paste   pg 116

ENDNOTE

see Footnotes and Endnotes   pg 59

ENVELOPES

You can create a single envelope with delivery and return address information or multiple envelopes using the mail merge feature.

Create an Envelope

1. Choose **Tools, Envelopes and Labels; Envelopes** tab.

2. Type in the **Delivery address** and the **Return address**. If there is already an address in the current document, it will automatically appear as the delivery address.

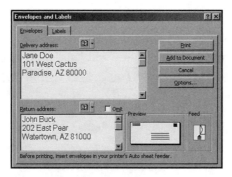

3. Click the **Print** button to print the envelope.

Alter Envelope Options

1. Choose **Tools, Envelopes and Labels; Envelopes** tab.

2. Click the **Options** [Options...] button to open the Envelope Options tab or click the **Preview** option.

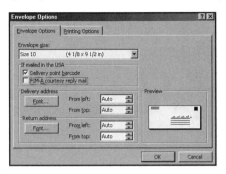

3. Alter the **Envelope size** and the address fonts as necessary. In addition, you can check the following:

   ■ **Delivery point barcode**—Prints the POSTNET bar code in a machine-readable representation of the zip code and delivery address, which will help your envelope reach its destination faster.

   ■ **FIM-A courtesy reply mail**—Prints a Facing Identification Mark, which is used to identify the front of a courtesy reply mail envelope during pre-sorting.

4. Click the **OK** [OK] button to accept your changes.

Alter Printing Options

1. Choose **Tools, Envelopes and Labels; Envelopes** tab.

2. Click the **Options** [Options...] button; **Printing Options** tab or click on the **Feed** area.

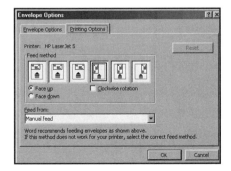

3. Select the **Feed method** you prefer to use with your printer or use the default setting selected automatically for your installed printer.

4. Click the **OK** [OK] button to accept your changes.

5. Click the **Print** [Print] button to print the envelope.

Quick Tips

Feature	Keyboard Shortcut
Mail Merge Check	(Alt)+(Shift)+(K)
Mail Merge Edit Data Source	(Alt)+(Shift)+(E)
Mail Merge to Document	(Alt)+(Shift)+(N)
Mail Merge to Printer	(Alt)+(Shift)+(M)

D
E
F

Create Mail Merge Envelopes

1. Choose **Tools**, **Mail Merge** to open the Mail Merge Helper dialog box.

2. Click the **Create** [Create ▾] button and choose **Envelopes** from the drop-down list in the **Main document** area.

3. Click the **New Main Document** [New Main Document] button to create a new main document.

4. Click the **Get Data** [Get Data ▾] button in the **Data Source** area, select an option from the drop-down list according to your data, and follow these steps:

  - **Create Data Source**—Opens the Create Data Source dialog box where you can add, remove, or change the order of your data source fields. Click the **OK** [OK] button to return to the Mail Merge Helper dialog box. Type a name for your mailing list source data document and click **Save** [🖫 Save] in the Save As dialog box. Word will inform you that the created data source is empty, so you will need to click the **Edit Data Source** [Edit Data Source] button to begin adding information to the data source fields in the Data Form dialog box (use the (Tab⇆) key to move between fields). Click the **Add New** [Add New] button each time you add data for a new entry. Click the **OK** [OK] button when finished. Then, click the **Mail Merge Helper** 🖼 button to return to the Mail Merge Helper dialog box, click the **Setup** [Setup...] button, and continue with the process at step 6.

■ **Open Data Source**—Opens the Open Data Source dialog box where you can select a previously created document that contains the fields to use as your data source and click the **Open** 🖅 Open button.

■ **Use Address Book**—Opens the Use Address Book dialog box where you can select the address book that you can use to insert fields as a data source (for example, **Outlook Address Book**) and click the **OK** [OK] button.

5. Click the **Set Up Main Document** [Set Up Main Document] button to set up your envelope document and open the Envelope Options dialog box.

6. Choose the desired **Envelope size**, select the **Delivery address** and **Return address** fonts, and click the **OK** [OK] button to accept the changes and open the Envelope Address dialog box.

7. Click the **Insert Merge Field** [Insert Merge Field ▾] drop-down button and select from the list of fields you want to insert into the envelope. Repeat this for each field you want—make sure you add spaces, commas, and press (↵Enter) to start new lines—on the envelope. You can delete any field or text using the (◆Backspace) key.

8. (Optional) Click the **Insert Postal Bar Code** Insert Postal Bar Code... button, which will open the Insert Postal Bar Code dialog box. This is where you can select either the **Merge field with ZIP code** or **Merge field with street address** drop-down lists to select the field in your label that Word will use to insert a POST-NET bar code on your envelope.

9. Click the **OK** OK button to accept the sample label you have created.

10. (Optional) Click the **Query Options** Query Options... button to open the Query Options dialog box. From here you can sort or filter your records according to the following tabs:

- **Filter Records**—Click one or more of the **Field** drop-down lists to select specific field(s) you want to separate out. For example, set **Field:** Home_State; **Comparison:** Equal to; **Compare to:** IN. Use the **And/Or** drop-down list to compound the filter requirements as necessary.

- **Sort Records**—Click up to three data fields that you want to use to organize your records. For example, set **Sort by:** Last_Name in **Ascending** order.

Click the **OK** OK button to accept the changes to the Query Options dialog box. You can also click the **Clear All** Clear All button in either tab to remove the sort or filter.

11. (Optional) Click the **Edit** Edit ▾ button and select the **Envelope: Document** if you want to add a return address to all your envelopes. Then, click the **Mail Merge Helper** button to return to the Mail Merge Helper dialog box.

Mail Merge Helper button

12. Click the **Merge** [Merge...] button on the Mail Merge Helper dialog box to open the Merge dialog box.

Send the envelope to a New document, Printer, or Electronic mail.

Available when using the Merge to Electronic mail option

Begin the merge process.

Cancel the merge process.

Choose how to report any errors that occur in the merge.

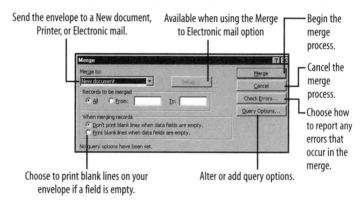

Choose to print blank lines on your envelope if a field is empty.

Alter or add query options.

13. Click the **Merge** [Merge] button in the Merge dialog box. Word creates a new Envelopes document that contains all the merged envelopes (if you selected to send the envelopes to a New document).

14. Click the **Save** 🖫 button to save the Envelopes document; click the **Print** 🖨 button to print the mail merged envelopes.

See Also Labels, Mail Merge

EXCEL WORKSHEETS

If you don't want to create a Word table in your document, you can embed an Excel worksheet directly in your document.

Quick Tip	
Feature	*Keyboard Shortcut*
Update Source	Ctrl + ⇧Shift + F7

Insert a New Embedded Excel Worksheet

1. Place the cursor in the document where you want to insert the worksheet.

2. Click the **Insert Microsoft Excel Spreadsheet** 🖾 button on the Standard toolbar and select the desired number of rows and columns.

3. Type in the data when the worksheet appears in the document.

TIP

If you want to link to an Excel workbook in your document, refer to the section on Objects. If you want to update a link to an Excel workbook in your document, refer to the section on Links.

Edit an Embedded Worksheet

1. Double-click directly on the worksheet in your document.

2. Edit the data as necessary; you can even click and drag the worksheet to a larger or smaller size.

3. Click in the Word document to return to working in the document and accept your worksheet edits.

Create a Chart with an Embedded Worksheet

1. Double-click directly on the worksheet in your document. Notice that the Standard toolbar becomes the Excel Standard toolbar.

2. Click the **Chart Wizard** 📊 button on the Standard toolbar.

3. Follow the wizard steps to create a chart and click the **Finish** ⬚Finish⬚ button when you are done.

See Also Charts, Files, Links, Objects, Tables

EXIT WORD

When you no longer want to work in Word, exit the application and return to the Windows desktop.

Quick Tip		
Feature	*Button*	*Keyboard Shortcut*
Exit	❎	Alt + F4

Exit Word

1. Click the **Close** ❎ button in the upper-right corner of the application window. You are asked whether you want to save your work.

2. Click the **Yes** ⬚Yes⬚ button to save your work (refer to **Save Documents** if you have problems saving your work); click the **No** ⬚No⬚ button to lose any unsaved

changes; or click the **Cancel** button to return to
working in the document.

See Also Save Documents, Start Word

EXPORT DOCUMENTS
see Save Documents   pg 128

FAX

Faxing a document is as easy as printing a document. Keep
in mind that you must have fax software installed on your
computer and an outgoing phone line.

Send an Office Document as a Fax

1. Choose **File**, **Print** to open the Print dialog box.
2. Select **Microsoft Fax** (or whatever fax software you
   have installed) from the **Printer Name** drop-down list.
3. Select the print to fax options (**Print range**, **Copies**,
   and **Print what**).
4. Click the **OK** button to send the fax.
   Depending on your fax software, you will be prompted
   to enter the phone number you want to fax to, recipient name, and a fax cover letter if necessary.

TIP

You can choose **File, New; Letters & Faxes** tab to create a fax
from a Word template or wizard.

See Also Help, Print

FIELDS
see Forms   pg 61

FILES

Instead of copying and pasting text and pictures into documents, you can insert an entire file.

Insert a File into a Document

1. Choose **Insert**, **File** to open the Insert File dialog box.

2. Select the **File name** and click the **Insert** [⮰ Insert ▾] button. The text and objects from the selected file are inserted directly into, and are now part of, your document.

Insert a Picture File

1. Choose **Insert**, **Picture**, **From File** to open the Insert Picture dialog box.

2. Select the **File name** and click the **Insert** [⮰ Insert ▾] button. The picture from the selected file is inserted directly into, and is now part of, your document.

TIP

You can resize and work with the picture file the same way you resize objects. See the section on Objects for more information.

See Also Hyperlinks, Objects

FIND FILES

Word allows you to set specific criteria for locating files for which you cannot remember the filename. You can perform all types of file searches, not only searches for Word documents.

Find a File

1. Click the **Open** [⮰] button to open the Open dialog box.

2. Click the **Tools** drop-down list at the top right of the dialog box and choose **Find**.

3. Click the **Look in** drop-down list box to look in a particular drive or folder. In the **Find files that match these criteria** section, you may choose to either look for a filename that will **Match all word forms** or **Match exactly**.

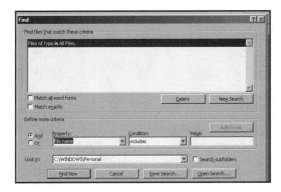

4. Click the **Property**, **Condition**, and **Value** drop-down list boxes in the **Define More Criteria** section to match a property (**File name**, **Comment**, **Author**, and so on) with a conditional value (**includes**, **begins with**, **ends with**).

5. Click the **Find Now** button to begin the search. If you cannot find the file, click the **New Search** button and try again.

See Also Open Document, Save Documents

FIND TEXT

You can use Word's Find feature to locate text, characters, paragraph formatting, or even special characters.

Quick Tip

Feature	*Button*	*Keyboard Shortcut*
Find	🔍	Ctrl + F
Browse Next		Ctrl + PgDn
Browse Previous		Ctrl + PgUp
Repeat Find		⬆Shift + F4 or Ctrl + Alt + Y

Find Regular Text

1. Choose **Edit, Find** to open the Find and Replace dialog box.
2. Type the text you want to locate into the **Find what** list box.
3. Click the **Find Next** ▭Find Next▭ button to move to each occurrence within the document. If there aren't any to be found, Word notifies you that it has finished searching the document and that the item wasn't found.

Perform an Advanced Search

1. Choose **Edit, Find** and click the **More** ▭More ✳▭ button to expand the **Search** options in the Find and Replace dialog box.
2. Type the text you want to locate in the **Find what** list box.
3. Select from the various **Search** options:
   - **Match case**—For example, instead of finding all occurrences of lowercased *sales*, you can search specifically for initial capped *Sales*.

- **Find whole words only**—For example, this will find *the* instead of also finding *them* and *they*.

- **Use wildcards**—For example, this will find character occurrences using the following *wildcards*: ? * [ ]. *R?t* will find *rot* and *rat*; *r*t* will find *replenishment* and *rut*; *r[ao]t* will find *rot*, *rat*, and *root*.

- **Sounds like**—For example, this will find phonetically similar text, such as *too*, *to*, and *two*.

- **Find all word forms**—For example, this will find different word forms, such as *eat*, *ate*, and *eaten*.

4. Select a specific **Format**, such as a particular **Font**; or **Special Characters**, such as a **Section Break**.

5. Click the **Find Next** ▢ Find Next ▢ button to move to each occurrence within the document. If no text or formats match your specific parameters, Word notifies you that it has finished searching the document and that the item wasn't found.

See Also Browse, Go To, Replace Text

FLOATING TOOLBAR
see Toolbars   pg 161

FONTS

To draw attention to important words and phrases in a document, you can change the text font options.

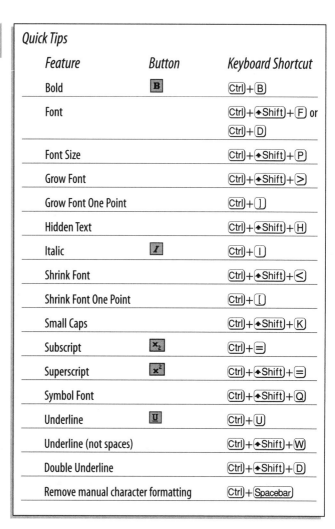

Quick Tips

Feature	Button	Keyboard Shortcut
Bold	`B`	`Ctrl`+`B`
Font		`Ctrl`+`Shift`+`F` or `Ctrl`+`D`
Font Size		`Ctrl`+`Shift`+`P`
Grow Font		`Ctrl`+`Shift`+`>`
Grow Font One Point		`Ctrl`+`]`
Hidden Text		`Ctrl`+`Shift`+`H`
Italic	`I`	`Ctrl`+`I`
Shrink Font		`Ctrl`+`Shift`+`<`
Shrink Font One Point		`Ctrl`+`[`
Small Caps		`Ctrl`+`Shift`+`K`
Subscript	`x₂`	`Ctrl`+`=`
Superscript	`x²`	`Ctrl`+`Shift`+`=`
Symbol Font		`Ctrl`+`Shift`+`Q`
Underline	`U`	`Ctrl`+`U`
Underline (not spaces)		`Ctrl`+`Shift`+`W`
Double Underline		`Ctrl`+`Shift`+`D`
Remove manual character formatting		`Ctrl`+`Spacebar`

Change Existing Text

1. Select the text that you want to draw attention to or place your cursor where you plan to type your text.

2. Click the **Font** drop-down list box on the Formatting toolbar and select the desired font.

3. Click the **Font Size** drop-down list box on the Formatting toolbar and select the desired font size.

4. Click the **Font Color** drop-down list box on the Formatting toolbar and select the desired font color.

Set the Default Font

1. Choose **Format**, **Font**; **Font** tab.
2. Select the font that you want to use as your default from the **Font** list box, and then click the **Default** `Default...` button.
3. Click the **Yes** `Yes` button in the message box to change the default font, which will affect all new documents in the Normal template.
4. Click the **OK** `OK` button to accept changes and return to the document.

Add Font Effects to Text

1. Select the text to which you want to add a font effect.
2. Choose **Format**, **Font**; **Text Effects** tab.
3. Select from the various types of **Effects**.
4. Click the **OK** `OK` button to accept changes and return to the document.

See Also Format Painter, Highlight Text, Text

FOOTNOTES AND ENDNOTES

Use a footnote at the end of a *page* to tell the reader the source of your information in a document. Use an endnote at the end of your *document* to cite research references.

Quick Tips	
Feature	*Keyboard Shortcut*
Footnote	Ctrl+Alt+F
Endnote	Ctrl+Alt+D

Insert a Footnote or Endnote

1. Click in the document where you want to insert the footnote or endnote number reference.

2. Choose **Insert**, **Footnote** to open the Footnote and Endnote dialog box.

3. Select the **Footnote** option to place the note at the end of the page, or the **Endnote** option to place the note at the end of the document.

4. Click the **OK** ⌷⌷ button to accept your selection. If you are in Print Layout view, you will be taken directly to where the footnote or endnote is to be inserted into your document. However, if you are in Normal view, you will be returned to the Footnotes or Endnotes window.

5. Type the text you want to appear as the footnote or endnote.

6. Click anywhere in the document when finished, if you are in Print Layout view. You must click the **Close** ⌷⌷ button to return to the document from the Footnotes or Endnotes window if you are working in Normal view.

Edit Footnote or Endnote

1. Double-click the footnote or endnote reference and type any changes; if you are in Print Layout view you may click directly on the footnote or endnote.

Delete Footnote or Endnote

1. Select the footnote or endnote reference in the text.

2. Press the Del key.

See Also Comments, Header and Footer, Views

FORMAT PAINTER

You can use the Format Painter to copy the formatting from a selected object or text and apply it to a different object or text you select.

Copy Character and Paragraph Formats

1. Select the text or object containing the format you want to duplicate.
2. Click the **Format Painter** ![icon] button on the Standard toolbar.
3. Select the text or object to reformat; it formats automatically.

Copy Formats to Multiple Locations

1. Select the text or object containing the format you want to duplicate.
2. Double-click the **Format Painter** ![icon] button on the Standard toolbar.
3. Select each particular text section or object to automatically format.
4. Click the **Format Painter** ![icon] button again when you are finished applying the format.

See Also Copy and Cut, Paste

FORMS

The Forms feature allows you to create a data entry form to ensure that the desired information can be entered into a document quickly and in a particular, consistent, and controlled format. You can create a form template and then save and print the information easily.

Create a Form

1. Click **New Blank Document** ![icon] on the Standard toolbar to make a new document into a form.
2. Choose **File**, **Save As** to open the Save As dialog box.

3. Click the **Save as type** drop-down list box and select **Document Template**. Notice that Word automatically selects the Templates folder as the default save location.

4. Type a **File name** for the template.

5. Click the **Save** ![Save button] button to save the template.

6. Choose **View, Toolbars, Forms** to display the Forms toolbar.

7. Click the **Insert Table** ![Insert Table icon] button and click the number of rows and columns you want in the table that will serve as the form entry area. If you want, set the form up in a document format, without the use of tables.

8. Type the field names in each cell and format the table as you like (see the Tables section for more information).

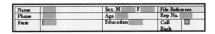

9. Place the cursor in the cell where you want to add a form field.

10. Click the appropriate **Form Field** button on the Forms toolbar to enter the form field:

   - **Text Form Field** ![abl icon] allows the user to input text into the form field.

   - **Check Box Form Field** ![check box icon] allows the user to select an option(s) listed as a form field.

   - **Drop-Down Form Field** ![drop-down icon] allows the user to select an option from a list of choices.

11. Repeat steps 9–10 for as many fields as you want on your form.

Set Drop-Down Form Field Options

1. Click a drop-down form field where you want to set the options and click the **Form Field Options** 🔄 button to open the Drop-Down Form Field Options dialog box.

2. Type in the **Drop-down item** text box the name for each of the possible fields and click the **Add** Add ▸▸ button after each entry.

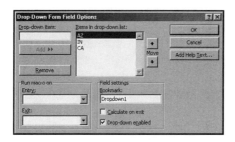

3. Click a particular item in the **Items in drop-down list** and click the **Remove** Remove button to delete the item.

4. Click the **OK** OK button to accept changes and return to the form.

Set Text Form Field Options

1. Click a text form field where you want to set the options and click the **Form Field Options** 🔄 button to open the Text Form Field Options dialog box.

2. Click the **Type** drop-down list to select the type of text to enter. Click the **Maximum length** spin box if you need to limit the size of the number.

3. Type an option in the **Default** (according to the type) text box in case the field doesn't have any input.

4. Click the **Format** (according to the type) drop-down list box to select the type of text.

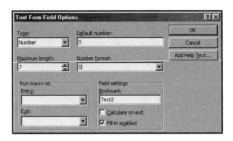

5. Click the **OK** <u>OK</u> button to accept changes and return to the form.

Set Check Box Form Field Options

1. Click a check box form field where you want to set the options and click the **Form Field Options** 🖼 button to open the Check Box Form Field Options dialog box.

2. Set the **Check box size** as either **Auto** or **Exactly** a point size using the spin box control.

3. Select the **Default value** as either **Checked** or **Not checked**.

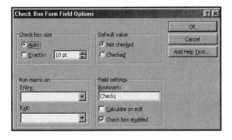

4. Click the **OK** <u>OK</u> button to accept changes and return to the form.

Finalizing the Form

1. Click the **Protect Form** 🔒 button on the Forms toolbar to protect the form from any changes.

2. Click the **Save** 💾 button on the Standard toolbar to save your form template.

3. Choose **File, Close** to close the form document template.

Use the Created Form

1. Choose **File, New; General** tab to open the New dialog box.

2. Double-click the document template you created to open the form as a document.

3. Enter the information in the form and click **Save** 🖫 on the Standard toolbar to save the document or click **Print** 🖨 to print the document form.

TIP

You can edit the created form *document* by opening up the file and saving any changes. In order to make changes to the original form *template*, you must open the template (see the section Edit a Created Form Template).

Edit a Created Form Template

1. Click **Open** 🖼 on the Standard toolbar to open the Open dialog box.

2. Click the **Look in** drop-down list box to help locate the correct file or drive (most likely the default **Templates** folder—try \Windows\Application Data\Microsoft\Templates). You can also click the **Up One Folder** 🖆 button to move through the folders.

3. Double-click the template file you want to open and Word opens the document template form.

4. Enter the information in the form and click **Save** 🖫 on the Standard toolbar to save the document template form.

See Also Tables, Templates

FRAMES

Word provides a frames feature that lets you organize your documents and Web documents into separate sections of information. You can use document frames to position note reference marks, comment marks, and fields; or Web frames to make Web pages easier to read and maneuver through.

Insert Document Text Box Frames

1. Click **Drawing** 📝 on the Standard toolbar to open the Drawing toolbar.

2. Click **Text Box** 📄 and draw the text box in the desired location in your document; make sure the text box is still selected.

3. Choose **Format, Text Box; Text Box** tab to open the Format Text Box dialog box.

4. Click the **Convert to Frame** `Convert to Frame...` button, which will open a message box asking you if you want to convert the drawing object to a frame (which might cause some formatting to be lost). Click the **OK** `OK` button to continue.

5. Type the text or place any objects in the text box and position the text box frame in your document.

Format Document Frames

1. Click to select the frame in your document.

2. Choose **Format, Frame** to open the Frame dialog box.

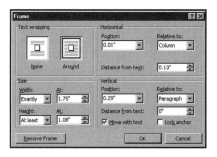

3. Select from the various **Text wrapping, Size, Horizontal,** and **Vertical** frame options.

4. Click the **OK** `OK` button to accept the changes and return to working in the document.

Remove Document Frames

1. Click to select the frame in your document.

2. Choose **Format, Frame** to open the Frame dialog box.

3. Click the **Remove Frame** [Remove Frame] button and the frame is removed (along with the text box), leaving the regular text or objects with a border around it.

Delete Document Frames

1. Click to select the text box frame in your document.

2. Press the Del key to delete the frame completely.

Insert Web Frames

1. Open a document or create a new document and choose **File, Save as Web Page**. Type the **File name** and click the **Save** [Save] button.

2. Choose **Format, Frames, New Frames Page** to establish the current frame and open the Frames toolbar.

3. Place the cursor in a frame where you want to add a new frame to the left, right, above, or below the current frame and click the appropriate button on the Frames toolbar.

4. Place the cursor in the frame that contains the content you want to have created into a table of contents. Click the **Table of Contents in Frame** 🔲 button to add a frame that organizes the contents of your Web document according to Word Heading styles. Click the **Save** [Save] button if you are asked to save any changes in your document.

5. Click the **Close** ⊠ button to close the Frames toolbar, or choose **View, Toolbars, Frames** to toggle the toolbar closed.

Alter Web Frame Properties

1. Click in the Web document frame where you want to alter the properties.

2. Choose **View, Toolbars, Frames** to open the Frames toolbar (if it isn't already open).

3. Click the **Frame Properties** 🔳 button on the Frames toolbar to open the Frame Properties dialog box.

4. Click the **Frame** tab and select the following options:

   - **Initial page**—type the initial page, site, or document to display when the frames page is opened.

   - **Link to file**—automatically updates the frame to any changes made in the linked document.

   - **Name**—assign a name to each frame.

   - **Size**—assign the specific **Width** and **Height** of the frame.

5. Click the **Borders** tab and select from the **Frames page** and **Individual frame** border width, color, and scrollbar options.

6. Click the **OK** [OK] button to accept the changes and return to working in the Web document.

Delete Web Frames

1. Click in the Web document frame that you want to delete.

2. Choose **View**, **Toolbars**, **Frames** to open the Frames toolbar (if it isn't already open).

3. Click the **Delete Frame** 🗙 button on the Frames toolbar to delete a frame.

See Also Background, Text Box, Themes, Web Pages

GO TO

You can use the Go To option in Word to browse your documents by moving through occurrences of selected items such as comments, bookmarks, footnotes, headings, and so on.

Use Go To

1. Choose **Edit**, **Go To** to open the Go To dialog box.

2. Click the **Go to what** item from the list box. The default browse item will be any item in the **Enter** list box. You can enter a **+** or **-** and a number to move the number of items relative to your current location. Or, you can simply type in or select the specific item from the list.

3. Click the **Next** ⌷Next⌷ button to move to the forward occurrence or the **Previous** ⌷Previous⌷ button to move to the backward occurrence.

4. Click the **Close** ⌷Close⌷ button when finished using the Go To dialog box.

See Also Browse, Find Text, Replace Text

GRAMMAR
see Spelling and Grammar   pg 132

GRAPHICS
see Drawing Tools   pg 41

HANGING INDENTS
see Indents   pg 79

G
H
I

HEADER AND FOOTER

Headers and footers are text that prints at the top and/or bottom of every page in a document—headers at the top, footers at the bottom. In addition, you can edit headers/footers, add different first page headers/footers, and add different odd and even headers/footers.

Insert Header and Footer

1. Choose **View, Header and Footer** to open the Header and Footer toolbar. Word automatically places the cursor in the Header area and displays the Header and Footer toolbar.

2. Type the text you want to print at the top of the page.

TIP

You can add graphical objects like clip art or WordArt to a header or footer. Refer to the appropriate section for information on how to insert these types of elements.

---

3. Click the **Header/Footer** 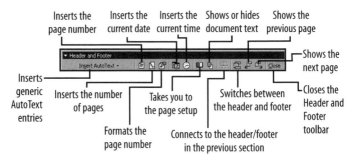 button on the Header and Footer toolbar to toggle from the header to the footer.

Inserts the page number · Inserts the current date · Inserts the current time · Shows or hides document text · Shows the previous page · Shows the next page · Inserts generic AutoText entries · Inserts the number of pages · Takes you to the page setup · Switches between the header and footer · Closes the Header and Footer toolbar · Formats the page number · Connects to the header/footer in the previous section

4. Double-click in the header or footer section to insert the cursor at a particular alignment and click any buttons on the toolbar to insert additional information.

5. Click the **Close** button to return to the main document.

TIP

You can use the Tab↹ key within the header and footer to alter the text alignment.

Edit a Header or Footer

1. Choose **View**, **Header and Footer** to open the Header and Footer toolbar. Word automatically places the cursor in the Header area and displays the Header and Footer toolbar.

2. Type any changes to the header by adding or deleting information. In addition, you can click on any other elements (graphics, and so on) in your header to select them to modify or delete them.

3. Click the **Header/Footer** button on the Header and Footer toolbar to toggle from the header to the footer and edit the footer information.

Add a Different First Page Header/Footer

1. Choose **View**, **Header and Footer** to open the Header and Footer toolbar. Word automatically places the

cursor in the Header area and displays the Header and Footer toolbar.

2. Click the **Page Setup** 🔲 button on the Header and Footer toolbar to open the Page Setup dialog box to the **Layout** tab.

3. Click either or both of the following **Headers and Footers** options:

   ■ **Different odd and even**—Allows you to create a different header or footer for even-numbered and odd-numbered pages.

   ■ **Different first page**—Allows you to create a different header or footer for the first page of a document or section.

4. Click the **OK** ⬛ OK button to accept the changes and return to entering the header and footer information.

5. Type the text or enter the elements you want in your header and footer.

G H I

Odd or even page designation   Section number designation   Graphical clip art element

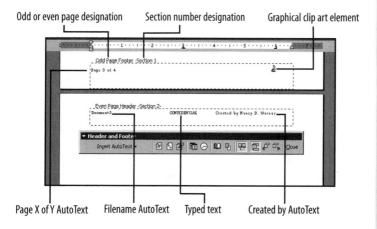

Page X of Y AutoText   Filename AutoText   Typed text   Created by AutoText

6. Click the **Close** button to save the header and footer changes and return to the document.

See Also AutoText, Page Numbers, Page Setup, Print Preview, Views

HELP

You can get help in Word 2000 in a couple of different ways. The Help Contents option is similar to using the table of contents in a book. The Answer Wizard option behaves similarly to the Office Assistant where you ask questions and it searches for related topics. The Help Index option lets you type the word or phrase you want to find and then view a list of all matching topics. What's This? Help offers a ScreenTip command with concise information about the command's function.

Quick Tips		
Feature	Button	Keyboard Shortcut
Help	?	F1
What's This?		⬆Shift)+F1

Get Contents Help

1. Press the F1 key and click the **Contents** tab.

2. Click the **+** of a topic to list all the subtopics. Click a subtopic to see the information displayed in the description area.

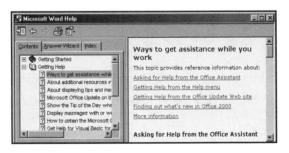

3. Click the **Close** ✖ button to exit Help.

TIP

If a word or phrase is underlined, it means that you can display a pop-up definition for the term. Point to the term and click the mouse button. A definition appears.

Get Answer Wizard Help

1. Press the **F1** key; **Answer Wizard** tab.
2. Type in your question.

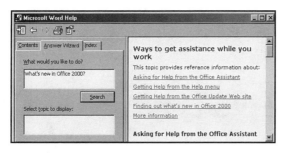

3. Click the **Search** button and select the topic from the frame on the right that you want to display.
4. Click the **Close** ✕ button to exit Help.

Get Index Help

1. Press the (F1) key; **Index** tab.
2. Type in a keyword and click the **Search** button.

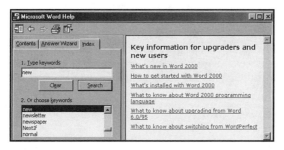

3. Select the topic you want in the description area.
4. Click the **Close** ✕ button to exit Help.

Print Help Topics

1. Select the Help item you want to print.
2. Click the **Print** 🖨 button on the toolbar.

Use What's This?

1. Choose **Help, What's This?** and the mouse pointer becomes a question mark pointer.
2. Click the command or object you want explained and read the What's This? pop-up.
3. Click anywhere in your workspace, or press the (Esc), (Alt), or (F10) keys to clear the pop-up information.

See Also Detect and Repair, Office Assistant, Office on the Web

HIGHLIGHT TEXT

When you want to draw attention to important text, highlight it. Highlighting is different from setting text color because you are altering the color of the text's background, not the text itself.

Highlight Existing Text

1. Select the text that you want to highlight.
2. Click the **Highlight** 🖊 drop-down list box on the Formatting toolbar and select the desired color; click **None** to have no highlight.

TIP

Keep in mind that highlight colors print as shades of gray unless you use a color printer; so don't use too dark a highlight color if you are printing to a non-color printer.

See Also Shading

HYPERLINKS

When you click a hyperlink, the document appears to *jump* to the related location. A hyperlink is an active link to a file, location, or element you want to move to.

Quick Tip		
Feature	*Button*	*Keyboard Shortcut*
Hyperlink		Ctrl + K

Type a URL Hyperlink into a Document

1. Click the mouse pointer in the document where you want to add the hyperlink.

2. Type the URL into your document and press ↵Enter; the address automatically becomes a hyperlink.

3. Move the mouse pointer over the hyperlink and the location of the hyperlink's destination displays in a ScreenTip.

> **TIP**
>
> If you aren't using the AutoFormat feature in Word that automatically formats URLs as hyperlinks, choose **Tools, AutoCorrect; AutoFormat** tab and select the **Replace** option of **Internet and network paths with hyperlinks.** Click the **OK** ok button to accept your changes and return to your document.

Insert a Hyperlink

1. Select the text that you want to convert to a hyperlink.

2. Click the **Insert Hyperlink** button on the Standard toolbar to open the Insert Hyperlink dialog box. Click the **Existing File or Web Page** option.

3. Type the link into the **Type the file or Web page name** text box, and select a link from the **Recent Files, Browsed Pages,** or **Inserted Links** list.

76

Files recently worked on

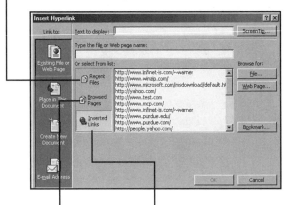

Web pages recently browsed Links recently used

G
H
I

4. Click the **OK** ok button to accept changes and
return to the document.

Insert a Document Hyperlink

1. Select the text that you want to make into a document
hyperlink.
2. Click the **Hyperlink** button on the Standard toolbar to open the Insert Hyperlink dialog box.
3. Click the **Existing File or Web Page** option.
4. Click the **Recent Files** option to see files you recently
worked on.
5. Select a link from the list box and click the **OK**
ok button to insert the hyperlink.

Insert an Email Hyperlink

1. Select the text that you want to make into an email
hyperlink.
2. Click the **Hyperlink** button on the Standard toolbar to open the Insert Hyperlink dialog box.
3. Click the **E-mail Address** option to make the link an
email address.

Alter a Hyperlink

1. Right-click a hyperlink and choose **Hyperlink**, **Edit Hyperlink** to open the Edit Hyperlink dialog box.
2. Click the **File** [File...] button to select a different linked file.
3. Double-click the file you want to link to.
4. Click the **OK** [OK] button to accept the edits.

> **TIP**
>
> In addition to changing a linked file when you alter a hyperlink, you can alter the text that is displayed in the **Text to display** text box, the type of link (Web page, document, email), or any other options in the Edit Hyperlink dialog box.

Edit Hyperlink ScreenTips

1. Right-click a hyperlink and choose **Hyperlink**, **Edit Hyperlink** to open the Edit Hyperlink dialog box.
2. Click the **ScreenTip** [ScreenTip...] button.
3. Type in the text you want the hyperlink ScreenTip to display.
4. Click the **OK** [OK] button in each dialog box to accept the changes. When you move the mouse pointer over the hyperlink, the new ScreenTip displays.

Remove a Hyperlink

1. Right-click a hyperlink and choose **Hyperlink**, **Remove Hyperlink**.

See Also Objects, Save Documents, Text, Web Pages

HYPHENATION

You can hyphenate words or phrases automatically or manually. In addition, use optional hyphens to control a break at the end of a line; and nonbreaking hyphens to prevent a hyphen breaking at the end of a line.

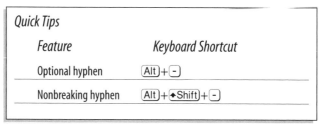

Quick Tips

Feature	Keyboard Shortcut
Optional hyphen	`Alt`+`-`
Nonbreaking hyphen	`Alt`+`⬆Shift`+`-`

Hyphenate Text Automatically

1. Choose **Tools, Language, Hyphenation** to open the Hyphenation dialog box.

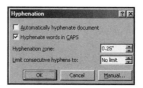

2. Select the **Automatically hyphenate document** option. Alter the **Hyphenation zone** if you like (the amount of space between the end of the last word and the margin) and **Limit consecutive hyphens to** to avoid *running* hyphens.

3. Click the **OK** button to return to the document.

Hyphenate Text Manually

1. Select all or part of the document to review the hyphenation.

2. Choose **Tools, Language, Hyphenation** to open the Hyphenation dialog box. If you select only one word, the particular word appears with the default hyphenation options listed.

3. Click the **Manual** button. Word moves through the document and asks whether certain words are to be hyphenated; click the **Yes** and **No** buttons as necessary (or the **Cancel** button to end at any time).

Insert an Optional Hyphen

1. Click in the location where you want to insert the optional hyphen.
2. Press Alt + ⬆Shift + -.

Insert a Nonbreaking Hyphen

1. Click in the location where you want to insert the nonbreaking hyphen.
2. Press Alt + ⬆Shift + -.

See Also AutoCorrect, AutoFormat

IMPORT FILES
see Open Document   pg 107

G
H
I

INDENTS

You can indent a line, paragraph, or multiple paragraphs in a document to the right of the left margin to make text stand out.

Quick Tips

Feature	Button	Keyboard Shortcut
Increase Indent	📇	Ctrl + M
Decrease Indent	📇	Ctrl + ⬆Shift + M
Hanging Indent		Ctrl + T
Un-indent		Ctrl + ⬆Shift + M
Un-hang		Ctrl + ⬆Shift + T

Increase and Decrease Indent

1. Select the text you want to indent.
2. Click the **Increase Indent** 📇 button to increase the text indent 1/2 inch at a time.
3. Click the **Decrease Indent** 📇 button to decrease the text indent 1/2 inch at a time.

Insert an Indent

1. Select the text you want to indent.
2. Click the Tab and indents setting at the left end of the horizontal ruler to toggle through and choose the type of indent.
3. Move the mouse pointer over the ruler where you want to place the indent, and click once directly on the ruler.

Remove an Indent

1. Click in the paragraph where you want to remove an indent.
2. Click the black indent marker on the horizontal ruler and drag it flush with the left margin edge.

Create a Hanging Indent

1. Select the text where you want to create a hanging indent.
2. Click the Tab and indents setting at the left end of the horizontal ruler and toggle through to choose **Hanging Indent** ; this will move all but the first line of a paragraph to the right.
3. Move the mouse pointer to the place on the ruler where you want the indent, and click once.

Create a First Line Indent

1. Select the text you want to give a first line indent.
2. Click the Tab and indents setting at the left end of the horizontal ruler and toggle through to choose **First Line Indent** ; this will move the first line of a paragraph to the right.
3. Move the mouse pointer to the place on the ruler where you want the indent, and click once.

TIP

You can move an indent by clicking the indent marker on the ruler and dragging it left or right to the desired location on the ruler.

See Also Alignment, Page Setup, Tabs

INDEX

Word can build and display an index in your document after you mark index entries (throughout your document) and choose the index design options. Word sorts the index entries alphabetically, references their page numbers, finds and removes duplicate entries from the same page, and displays the index in the document.

Quick Tip

Feature	*Keyboard Shortcut*
Mark Index Entry	(Alt)+(⬆Shift)+(X)

G
H
I

Mark Index Entries

1. Select the text you want to serve as an index entry.

2. Press (Alt)+(⬆Shift)+(X) to open the Mark Index Entry dialog box.

3. Click the **Mark All**  button to mark all entries of the selected text as a main entry in the document.

4. Repeat steps 1 and 3; the Mark Index Entry dialog box remains open until you click the **Close** Close button when you have finished marking all the index entries.

Create the Index

1. Place the cursor at the location in the document where you want to create the index.

2. Choose **Insert, Index and Tables; Index** tab after you have marked all your index entries.

3. Select the **Right align page numbers** option and set the **Columns** spin box to **1**.

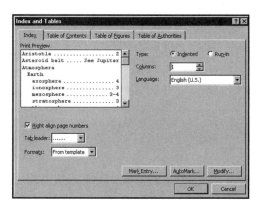

4. Click the **OK** button to accept changes and create the index.

See Also AutoSummarize, Table of Contents

INSERT FILE
see Files   pg 53

ITALICS
see Text   pg 155

JUSTIFICATION
see Alignment   pg 3

LABELS

Word can help you create and print either one label or multiple labels for a mass mailing.

Create a Label

1. Choose **Tools, Envelopes and Labels; Labels** tab.

2. Type the text you want on the label in the **Address** text box. Or, click the **Address Book** button to select from your address book.

3. Select the **Print** option for whether you want a **Full page of the same label** or a **Single label**.

4. Click the **Options** button and select the **Label products** and **Product number**; or click directly on the **Label** area.

5. (Optional) Click the **New Document** button to see exactly what the labels will look like when printed. This is a good way to visually check that the label **Product number** you selected matches. In addition, you can save this document and use it again in the future instead of performing these steps.

6. Click the **OK** button to accept the changes.

7. Click the **Print** button to send the labels to the printer.

Quick Tips	
Feature	*Keyboard Shortcut*
Mail Merge Check	Alt + Shift + K
Mail Merge Edit Data Source	Alt + Shift + E
Mail Merge to Document	Alt + Shift + N
Mail Merge to Printer	Alt + Shift + M

84

Create Mail Merge Labels

1. Choose **Tools, Mail Merge** to open the Mail Merge Helper dialog box.

2. Click the **Create** [Create ▾] button and choose **Mailing Labels** from the drop-down list in the **Main document** area.

3. Click the **New Main Document** [New Main Document] button to create a new main document.

4. Click the **Get Data** [Get Data ▾] button in the **Data source** area, select an option from the drop-down list according to your data, and follow the steps:

   - **Create Data Source**—Opens the Create Data Source dialog box where you can add, remove, or change the order of your data source fields. Click the **OK** [OK] button to return to the Mail Merge Helper dialog box. Type a name for your mailing list source data document and click **Save** [Save] in the Save As dialog box. Word will inform you that the created data source is empty, so you will need to click the **Edit Data Source** [Edit Data Source] button to begin adding information to the data source fields in the Data Form dialog box (use the Tab↹ key to move between fields). Click the **Add New** [Add New] button each time you add data for a new entry. Click the **OK** [OK] button when finished. Then, click the **Mail Merge Helper** button to return to the Mail Merge Helper dialog box, and click the **Setup** [Setup...] button, and continue with the process at step 6.

   - **Open Data Source**—Opens the Open Data Source dialog box where you can select a previously created document that contains the fields to use as your data source; click the **Open** [Open] button.

   - **Use Address Book**—Opens the Use Address Book dialog box where you can select the address book that you can use to insert fields as a data source (for example, **Outlook Address Book**); click the **OK** [OK] button.

5. Click the **Set Up Main Document**
   [Set Up Main Document] button to set up your label document and open the Label Options dialog box.

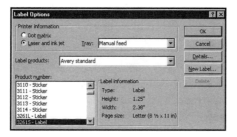

6. Choose the desired **Printer information**, **Label products**, and **Product number** for the labels and click the
   OK [OK] button to accept the changes and open
   the Create Labels dialog box.

7. Click the **Insert Merge Field** [Insert Merge Field ▾] drop-down
   button and select from the list of fields you want to
   insert into the label. Repeat this for each field you
   want—make sure you add spaces, commas, and press
   ↵Enter to start new lines—on the label. You can delete
   any field or text using the ←Backspace key.

8. (Optional) Click the **Insert Postal Bar Code**
   [Insert Postal Bar Code...] button, which will open the Insert
   Postal Bar Code dialog box. This is where you can
   select either the **Merge field with ZIP code** or **Merge
   field with street address** drop-down lists to select the
   field in your label that Word will use to insert a POST-
   NET bar code on your envelope.

J
K
L

9. Click the **OK** 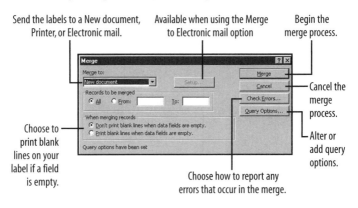 button to accept the sample label you have created.

10. (Optional) Click the **Query Options** button to open the Query Options dialog box. From here you can sort or filter your records according to the following tabs:

   ■ **Filter Records**—Click one or more of the **Field** drop-down lists to select specific field(s) you want to separate out. For example, set **Field:** Home_State; **Comparison:** Equal to; **Compare to:** IN. Use the **And/Or** drop-down list to compound the filter requirements as necessary.

   ■ **Sort Records**—Click up to three data fields that you want to use to organize your records. For example, set **Sort by:** Last_Name in **Ascending** order.

   Click the **OK** button to accept the changes to the Query Options dialog box. You can also click the **Clear All** button in either tab to remove the sort or filter.

11. Click the **Merge** button on the Mail Merge Helper dialog box to open the Merge dialog box.

Send the labels to a New document, Printer, or Electronic mail.

Available when using the Merge to Electronic mail option

Begin the merge process.

Choose to print blank lines on your label if a field is empty.

Cancel the merge process.

Alter or add query options.

Choose how to report any errors that occur in the merge.

12. Click the **Merge** ⬚ Merge ⬚ button in the Merge dialog box. Word creates a new Labels document that contains all the merged labels (if you selected to send the labels to a new document).

13. Click the **Save** 🖫 button to save the Label document; click the **Print** 🖨 button to print the mail merged labels.

See Also Envelopes, Mail Merge, Print

LANDSCAPE
see Page Setup   pg 112

LETTERS

Word's Letter Wizard helps you select letter options that will create a letter quickly and easily. Your letter will be based on frequently used styles and page designs.

Create a Letter with the Letter Wizard

1. Choose **Tools, Letter Wizard; Letter Format** tab.

2. Select the type of letter from the **Choose a page design** drop-down list box.

3. Select the style of letter from the **Choose a letter style** drop-down list box.

4. Click the **Pre-printed letterhead** check box if you want to use paper with a letterhead on it. Select from the **Where on the page is the letterhead?** drop-down list and the **How much space does the letterhead need?** spin box.

5. Click the **Recipient Info** tab and either enter the **Recipient's name** and **Delivery address** or select it by clicking the **Address Book** 🕮 button.

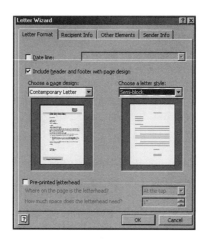

6. Select the type of **Salutation** you want the letter to begin with.

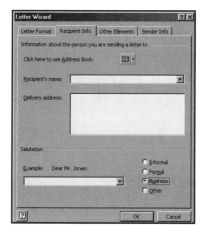

7. Click the **Sender Info** tab and enter the **Sender's name** and **Return Address** or select it by clicking the **Address Book** button.

8. Click the **OK** button to review the document and type your text into the letter.

TIP

Click the **Other Elements** tab to include Reference line, Mailing instructions, Attention, or Subject options.

See Also Envelopes, Labels, Mail Merge, Templates

LEFT ALIGN
see Alignment   pg 3

LINE NUMBERS

You can have line numbers in the entire or only a portion of your document. This is convenient when writing a script or legal document where you need to refer to specific lines in a document.

Add Document Line Numbers

1. Choose **File**, **Page Setup**; **Layout** tab.
2. Click the **Line Numbers** button to open the Line Numbers dialog box.
3. Click the **Add line numbering** check box and select from the other options:
   - **Start at**—The starting line number.
   - **From text**—The distance between the left edge of the document and the line number.
   - **Count By**—The amount by which you want to increment the line numbers.

- **Numbering**—Whether you want the line numbering to begin on a new page, a new section, or remain continuous throughout the document.

4. Click the **OK** [ok] button in both dialog boxes to accept changes and return to the document. Keep in mind that each time you press (⏎Enter), you create a new paragraph and begin a new line.

See Also Numbered Lists, Page Setup

LINE SPACING

Word allows you to set the amount of vertical space between lines of text.

Quick Tips

Feature	Button	Keyboard Shortcut
Line Spacing 1	▤	Ctrl+1
Line Spacing 1.5	▤	Ctrl+5
Line Spacing 2	▤	Ctrl+2

Alter Line Spacing

1. Select the text where you want to alter the line spacing. Or, you can alter the line spacing before you begin entering any text.

2. Choose **Format, Paragraph; Indents and Spacing** tab.

3. Click the **Line spacing** drop-down list box and select the size you want.

4. Click the **OK** [ok] button to accept changes and return to the document.

TIP

If you select the **Line spacing** options of **At least** or **Exactly**, you can use the **At** spin box control to set the font point size.

See Also Character Spacing, Fonts, Paragraph Spacing, Text

LINES

see Borders   pg 15

LINES OF TEXT

See Breaks   pg 18

LINKS

Objects and information in Word can be linked to other sources and files. You can easily update, open, or change the links to refer to different objects, files, and data.

Update a Link

1. Open the file that contains a linked object.

2. Choose **Edit**, **Links** to open the Links dialog box. Any linked **Source file** will be listed with the file and folder location.

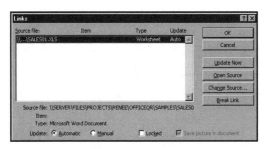

3. Click the **Update Now** Update Now button to update the link and click the **OK** OK button to return to the worksheet.

Open a Link Source

1. Open the file that contains a linked object.

2. Choose **Edit**, **Links** to open the Links dialog box. Any linked **Source file** will be listed with the file and folder location.

3. Click the **Open Source** Open Source button to open the linked file.

4. Make any changes to the workbook file and click the **Close** ⊠ button to return to the file containing the linked object; any changes will appear automatically.

J
K
L

Change a Link Source

1. Open the file that contains a linked object.

2. Choose **Edit, Links** to open the Links dialog box. Any linked **Source file** will be listed with the file and folder location.

3. Click the **Change Source** [Change Source...] button to change the linked filename in the Change Links dialog box.

4. Click the **Places bar** option for the location of the file you want to open.

5. Click the **Look in** drop-down list box to help locate the correct file or drive. You can also click the **Up One Level** [⬆] button to move through folders.

6. Double-click the file you want to open and Word updates the **Source file** in the Links dialog box. Click the **OK** [OK] button to return to the document with the updated link.

TIP

If you no longer want the link to update automatically in your docu-

ment, click the **Break Link** [Break Link] button. The data remains in your document, but will no longer update or be listed as a link in the Links dialog box.

See Also Objects, Paste

MACROS

You can create a macro that will accomplish just about any task. With the macro recording option, you can record and save your actions, and then these actions will be performed for you whenever you run the macro.

Quick Tip		
Feature	*Button*	*Keyboard Shortcut*
Macro	▶	Alt+F8

Create a Macro

1. Choose **Tools, Macro, Record New Macro** to open the Record Macro dialog box.

2. Type a name in the **Macro name** text box.

Assigns the macro you record to a toolbar button ——

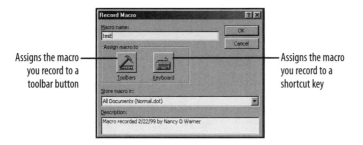

—— Assigns the macro you record to a shortcut key

3. Click the **OK** OK button. The Macro toolbar appears with the **Stop Recording** ■ and **Pause Recording** ⅠⅠ● buttons.

4. Perform any tasks that you want the macro to record and click the **Stop Recording** ■ button when finished.

TIP

Macros are also items that you can add to your toolbars to make it easy to launch them. Read the Toolbars section and follow along the steps of adding a button to your toolbar, but choose **Macros** from the **Categories** list. Then choose the specific macro in the **Commands** list.

Run a Macro

1. Press the Alt + F8 keys to open the Macros dialog box.

2. Double-click the **Macro name** and the macro will run.

Modify or Delete a Macro

1. Choose **Tools, Macro, Macros** to open the Macro dialog box.

2. Click the **Macro name** and click the appropriate button to perform the modification you desire:

   - **Edit**—Opens the Visual Basic editor to the macro code. Make any changes and click the **Close** ☒ button to return to your document.

- **Delete**—Asks if you want to delete the macro. Click the **Yes** [Yes] button to delete the macro. Click the **Close** [Close] button to return to your document.

See Also Find Text, Replace Text

MAIL MERGE

Word allows you to create a document that merges a letter (main document) with a list of addresses (data source). You can use the Mail Merge Helper to create the main document and the data source, insert the field names into the main document, and quickly and easily merge them together.

> **Quick Tips**
>
> | Feature | Keyboard Shortcut |
> | --- | --- |
> | Mail Merge Check | Alt + ↑Shift + K |
> | Mail Merge Edit Data Source | Alt + ↑Shift + E |
> | Mail Merge to Document | Alt + ↑Shift + N |
> | Mail Merge to Printer | Alt + ↑Shift + M |

Create the Main Document

1. Choose **Tools**, **Mail Merge** to open the Mail Merge Helper dialog box.

2. Click the **Create** [Create ▾] button and choose **Form Letters** from the drop-down list in the **Main document** area.

3. Click the **New Main Document** [New Main Document] button to create a new main document. Or, click **Active Window** [Active Window] if you already have a document open that you want to use for the merge.

4. Click the **Edit** [Edit ▾] button and select **Form Letter:** Document*x* (where *x* is the number that Word automatically gives the next open document).

5. Type the document the way you want the form letter to appear, leaving blank spaces where you want the merged data entered. Notice the Mail Merge toolbar is displayed, when you view your main document.

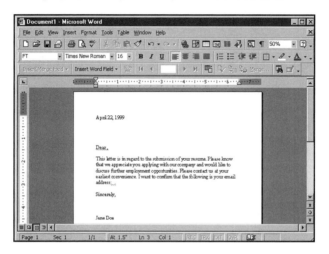

6. Choose **File, Save** to open the Save As dialog box. Assign a **File name** and click the **Save** 🖫 Save button to save the changes to your main document.

Get Data Source

1. Choose **Tools, Mail Merge** to open the Mail Merge Helper dialog box. You can also click the **Mail Merge Helper** 🖫 button to open the dialog box from the main document at any time.

2. Click the **Get Data** Get Data ▾ button in the **Data source** area, select an option from the drop-down list according to your data, and follow the steps:

   ■ **Create Data Source**—You will want to use this option when you need to create a data source from scratch. Selecting this option opens the Create Data Source dialog box where you can add, remove, or change the order of your data source fields. Click the **OK** ok button to return to the Mail Merge Helper dialog box. Type a name for your mailing list source data document and click **Save** 🖫 Save in the Save As dialog box. Word will inform you that the created data source is empty, so you will need to click the **Edit Data Source** [Edit Data Source] button to begin adding information to the data source fields in the Data Form dialog box (use the (Tab⁵) key to move between fields). Click the **Add New** [Add New] button each time you add data for a new entry. Click the **OK** [OK] button when finished, to return to the main document.

- **Open Data Source**—You will want to use this option when you need to open a file that contains the fields to use as your data source. Selecting this option opens the Open Data Source dialog box, where you can click on a previously created file and click the **Open** [Open] button.

- **Use Address Book**—You will want to use this option when you want to use a contacts list as your data source. Selecting this option opens the Use Address Book dialog box where you can select the address book that you can use to insert fields as a data source and click the **OK** [OK] button.

- **Header Option**—You will want to use a separate header source when you are using several data sources, when a data source doesn't contain a header record, or when the header field names don't match the merge field names in the main document. Selecting this option opens the Header Options dialog box:

    - If you already have a header source, choose the **Open** [Open] button, select the file to open, and click the **Open** [Open] button. Click the **Edit** [Edit ▼] button and select **Form Letter:** Document*x* to return to the main document.

    - If you don't have a header source, choose the **Create** [Create] button, add or remove field names for your header row, click the **OK** [OK] button, give the header source document a specific name, and click the **Save** [Save] button.

3. Click the **Edit Main Document** [Edit Main Document] button to view and edit the fields in your data source document (unless you are already in your main document); then save changes as necessary.

Insert Field Names

1. Place the cursor in the main document where you want to insert a merge field from the data source.

2. Click the **Insert Merge Field** [Insert Merge Field ▾] button on the Mail Merge toolbar and select from the list of fields you want to insert into the main document.

3. Repeat steps 1 and 2 for each field you want to insert into the main document.

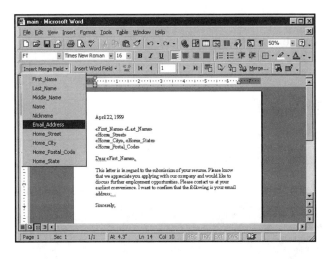

4. Click **Save** 🖫 on the Standard toolbar to save the main document now that it contains the source data fields.

Merge Documents

1. Click the **Merge** [Merge...] button on the Mail Merge toolbar.

2. Click the **Merge** [Merge] button in the Merge dialog box. Word creates a new Form Letters document that contains all the merged letters (if you selected to send the labels to a New document).

M
98

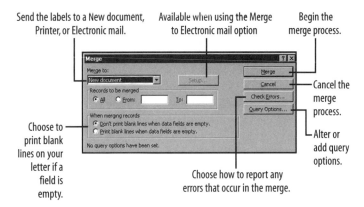

Send the labels to a New document, Printer, or Electronic mail.

Available when using the Merge to Electronic mail option

Begin the merge process.

Cancel the merge process.

Alter or add query options.

Choose to print blank lines on your letter if a field is empty.

Choose how to report any errors that occur in the merge.

3. Move through the merged document to verify the merged fields from the data to the main document.

4. Click the **Save** 🖫 button to save the Form Letters document; click the **Print** 🖨 button to print the mail merge.

See Also Envelopes, Labels, Letters, Templates

MAIL RECIPIENTS
see Email   pg 43

see Email   pg 43

MARGINS
see Page Setup   pg 112

see Page Setup   pg 112

MENUS

The menu bar is just below the title bar and the available commands vary depending on what you are doing in Word. You select commands on the menu to perform operations. Word 2000 now has a *personalized* menu option, which displays only those commands relevant to what you are doing in the document at that time.

Quick Tips	
Feature	*Keyboard Shortcut*
Menu Mode On	F10
Menu Mode On	Alt

Use Personalized Menus

1. Click the menu category that you want to open.

2. Click the drop-down arrow 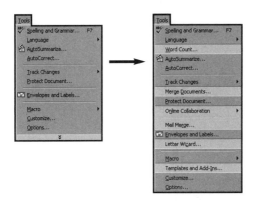 to show all the commands available.

3. Click the command on the menu you want and the menu closes automatically.

Use Regular Menus

1. Click the menu category that you want to open.

2. Click the command on the menu you want and the menu closes automatically.

Close a Menu Without Choosing a Command

1. Click the menu category that you want to open.

2. Click elsewhere on the desktop or press the (Esc), (Alt), or (F10) key to close the menu.

Turn Personalized Menus On/Off

1. Choose **Tools, Customize; Options** tab.

2. Select the **Menus show recently used commands first** option if you want to turn the personalized menus on. Deselect the option to turn them off.

3. Click the **Close** button to accept changes and return to the document.

See Also Dialog Boxes, Toolbars

M
N
O

MERGE DOCUMENTS

You can combine multiple documents into one main document as well as merge comments and changes.

Merge Documents

1. Open the main document into which you want to merge other documents and/or comments and changes.

2. Choose **Tools**, **Merge Documents** to open the Select File to Merge into Current Document dialog box.

3. Double-click the document you want to merge into the current document. If asked, click the **OK** [OK] button or the **Cancel** [Cancel] button if there are any untracked changes.

> **TIP**
> You can merge the comments or tracked changes in multiple documents by repeating steps 2 and 3.

See Also Comments, Track Changes

M
N
O

MOVE TEXT

You can reorganize text in a Word document by moving items as you work. This method can be faster than cutting and pasting text.

Move Text to a New Location

1. Select the text you want to move.

2. Press and hold down the left mouse button over the selected text, and drag the pointer to the new location.

3. Release the mouse button to drop the text in the new location.

See Also Copy and Cut, Objects, Paste

NEW DOCUMENT

Word presents a new blank document each time you start the application. You can create another new document at any time. In addition, Word provides templates and wizards that can help you create different types of new documents.

Quick Tip		
Feature	*Button*	*Keyboard Shortcut*
New Document	▭	Ctrl + N

Create a New Document

1. Click the **New** ▭ button on the Standard toolbar and Word opens a new document.

Use a New Document Template or Wizard

1. Choose **File**, **New** to open the New dialog box.

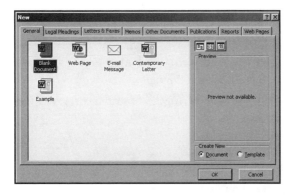

2. Select the tab that corresponds with the type of document you want to create and review the available options.

3. Double-click either the document template to begin inserting the new text or the document wizard and follow the steps, filling in the appropriate information as necessary:

- Click the **Next** `Next >` button to move through the wizard answering options.
- Click the **Finish** `Finish` button when you have completed the wizard.

TIP

When in the New dialog box, the **Create new** option will default to **Document**. If you select the **Template** option, you will create a new document template, which is covered in the section on Templates.

See Also Open Document, Styles, Templates

NORMAL VIEW
see Views   pg 168

NUMBERED LISTS

Numbered lists are useful for presenting a series of items when they need to be kept in sequential order.

Number New Text

1. Click the **Numbering** button on the Formatting toolbar and begin typing.
2. Click the **Numbering** button again when you have finished your list.

Number Existing Text

1. Select the text that you want to number.
2. Click the **Numbering** button on the Formatting toolbar. Notice that a number is added to each paragraph, not each sentence.

Alter Numbers

1. Select the numbered text you want to alter.
2. Choose **Format, Bullets and Numbering; Numbered** tab.
3. Double-click the type of numbers you want to display.

See Also Bulleted Lists, Outline

OBJECTS

A Word object can be any of numerous types of elements that you add to your document: file, art, chart, worksheet, photo, movie, text clip, and so on.

Insert a New Object

1. Choose **Insert, Object; Create New** tab.

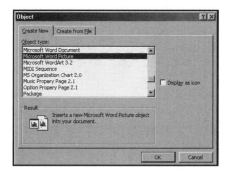

2. Click on the object type in the **Object type** list box.
3. Click the **OK** ![OK] button to accept changes and return to the document.
4. Click directly on the object and make any changes to it using the associated toolbar.

Insert an Object File

1. Choose **Insert, Object; Create from File** tab.
2. Type in the **File name** or click the **Browse** ![Browse...] button to select the file from a specific location.
3. Select the **Link to file** option if you want the object to be linked to this document and the source file. This means that any changes you make in the source file are reflected in your document.

M
N
O

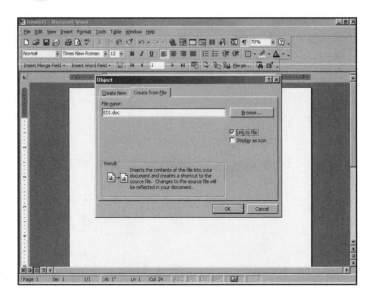

4. Click the **OK** [OK] button to accept changes and return to the document.

TIP

You can insert an existing Excel spreadsheet in a Word document to create a chart. For example, a monthly report might always need to include a chart that comes from up-to-date data that is kept in Excel.

Resize Objects

1. Click once directly on an object and the object handles appear on all sides and corners of the object.

2. Move the mouse pointer over one of the handles. When the pointer becomes a two-headed arrow, click and hold the handle.

3. Drag the handle to the desired size. If you drag from the corner handles, the height and width increase or decrease proportionately. Drag the handle on top to increase height and the handle on the side to increase width.

4. Click elsewhere in the document to deselect the object.

Move Objects

1. Click once directly on an object and the object handles appear on all sides and corners of the object.
2. Move the mouse pointer over the object. When the pointer appears with a gray box below it, click and hold the pointer.
3. Drag the object to the new location and drop the object.

Delete Objects

1. Click once directly on an object and the object handles appear on all sides and corners of the object.
2. Press the Del key and the object is removed from the document.

TIP

If you link a worksheet object in your document, you can quickly edit or open the source file by double-clicking the object. You can also copy, cut, and paste an object to a different location.

See Also Clip Art, Drawing Tools, Excel Worksheets

OFFICE ASSISTANT

The Office Assistant is the default way to search for help on a particular topic and find shortcuts in Word documents using normal, plain English questions. It helps you find instructions and tips for getting your work done more easily.

Quick Tip		
Feature	*Button*	*Keyboard Shortcut*
Help	?	F1

Show and Hide the Office Assistant

1. Choose **Help, Show the Office Assistant**.
2. Choose **Help, Hide the Office Assistant**.

Ask the Office Assistant Questions

1. Click on the **Assistant** character if it is onscreen; otherwise, click the **Help** 🔲 button on the Standard toolbar.

2. Type in the question or term for which you want information and click the **Search** 🔲 button.

3. Click the bullet next to the information you want and then select the topic you want Microsoft Office to reference.

4. Click the **Close** ⊠ button in the upper-right corner of the Help window to close the Help window.

5. Right-click the **Assistant** and click **Hide** from the shortcut menu. This simply hides the Assistant from the screen; see the section Turn the Assistant Off to make it go away completely.

Change the Assistant

1. Right-click the **Assistant** and click **Choose Assistant** from the shortcut menu.

2. Scroll through the different Assistant options using the **Next** 🔲 and **Back** 🔲 buttons in the Gallery page of the Office Assistant dialog box.

3. Click the **OK** 🔲 button when you finish selecting an Assistant.

Turn the Assistant Off

1. Right-click the **Assistant** and click **Options** from the shortcut menu.

2. Click to deselect the **Use the Office Assistant** option and click the **OK** 🔲 button.

See Also Detect and Repair, Help, Office on the Web

OFFICE ON THE WEB

Microsoft Office on the Web takes you to the Microsoft
Office Web site and provides you with access to download
free stuff, product news, updates, frequently asked questions,
online support, and many other ways to get information.

Microsoft Office Update Web Site

1. Choose **Help**, **Office on the Web**.

2. Peruse the Microsoft Office Web Site with your Web
   browser.

3. Click the **Close** ☒ button when you want to return to
   the document.

See Also Detect and Repair, Help, Office Assistant

OPEN DOCUMENT

Each time you want to work with a document, you need to
open it using the Open dialog box.

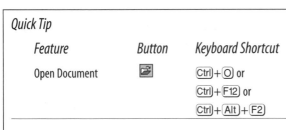

Quick Tip

Feature	Button	Keyboard Shortcut
Open Document	🖼	Ctrl+O or
		Ctrl+F12 or
		Ctrl+Alt+F2

M
N
O

Open a Document

1. Click the **Open** 🖼 button on the Standard toolbar to
   open the Open dialog box listing the saved Word documents.

2. Click the **Places bar** option for the location of the file you want to open.

3. Click the **Look in** drop-down list box to help locate the correct file or drive. You can also click the **Up One Folder** 🔁 button to move through folders.

4. Double-click the file you want to open and Word opens the document.

TIP

To preview the document before you open it, click the **Views** 🔳 drop-down button on the Open dialog box toolbar and select **Preview**. The document will display in the preview pane on the right side of the Open dialog box. The Open dialog box will stay in preview pane view until you alter the view again or exit Word.

Open Files of Different Type

1. Click the **Open** 📂 button on the Standard toolbar to open the Open dialog box listing the saved Word documents.

2. Click the **Files of type** drop-down list box and select the file type. The Open dialog box displays only files that are of the type you select. Then, locate the folder that contains the file you want to open.

3. Double-click the file you want to open and Word opens the document. If the file cannot be opened because there is a compatibility error, Word alerts you of this with a message box.

TIP

If you cannot open a file in Word, try opening the file in the application it was created in and copy and paste the information into a Word document. Or, you can try to save the file in the application as a Word document, similar to the section Save as a Different File Type.

See Also New Document, Templates

ORIENTATION
see Page Setup   pg 112

OUTLINE

Word's outline feature assigns preset styles to headings and
normal text. You can easily create an outline with the
Outlining toolbar.

Quick Tips

Feature	*Button*	*Keyboard Shortcut*
Outline Collapse	▬	Alt + ⬆Shift + - or Alt + ⬆Shift + - (Numeric keypad)
Outline Demote	➡	Alt + ⬆Shift + →
Outline Expand	✚	Alt + ⬆Shift + = or Alt + ⬆Shift + + (Numeric keypad)
Outline Move Down	⬇	Alt + ⬆Shift + ↓
Outline Move Up	⬆	Alt + ⬆Shift + ↑
Outline Promote	⬅	Alt + ⬆Shift + ←
Outline Show First Line	≣	Alt + ⬆Shift + L
Outline Show All		Alt + ⬆Shift + A

M
N
O

Create Outline

1. Click the **Outline View** 🖹 button to switch to
   Outline view. Or, choose **View**, **Outline**. The Outlining
   toolbar appears automatically.
2. Type in your text and click the Outlining toolbar buttons to alter your text as headings or normal text.

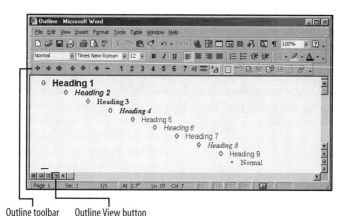

Outline toolbar   Outline View button

3. Save your document as you normally would and switch to alternative views if necessary.

See Also Fonts, Styles, Views, Workspace

PAGE BREAK
see Breaks   pg 18

PAGE NUMBERS

Word can automatically insert page numbers in your documents and print the page numbers in the position and format you specify. Note that page numbers are inserted as frames in your document, unlike headers and footers, though you can use headers and footers to add page numbers.

Insert Page Numbers

1. Choose **Insert**, **Page Numbers** to open the Page Numbers dialog box.

2. Click the **Position** drop-down arrow to select whether you want the page number at the top or bottom of the page.

3. Click the **Alignment** drop-down arrow to select whether you want the page number at the left, center, or right side of the page, or on the inside or outside of the page.

4. Click the **OK** `OK` button to accept changes and return to the document. You can see the page number (grayed out) in Print Layout view.

TIP

If you don't want a page number on the first page, click to remove the check mark from the **Show number on first page** check box of the Page Numbers dialog box.

Alter Page Number Format

1. Choose **Insert, Page Numbers** to open the Page Numbers dialog box.
2. Click the **Format** `Format...` button to open the Page Number Format dialog box.
3. Click the **Number format** drop-down list box and select from the options available.
4. Click the **Include chapter number** check box if you want to include a chapter number with the page number. Then you can choose from the following options:

    - **Chapter starts with style** drop-down list to select the heading number that indicates a new chapter.
    - **Use separator** drop-down list box to separate the chapter and page number with a **hyphen, period, colon, em-dash,** or **en-dash.**

5. Click the **Page numbering** option to either **Continue from previous section** or **Start at** a particular page number.
6. Click the **OK** `OK` button in each dialog box to accept changes and return to the document.

See Also Header and Footer, Views

P
Q
R

PAGE SETUP

You can adjust the page margins, orientation, paper size, and paper source for documents. All of these settings can be applied to a particular section, an entire document, or from the current cursor point forward.

Set Margins

1. Choose **File, Page Setup; Margins** tab. You can also double-click the gray area of the horizontal ruler.

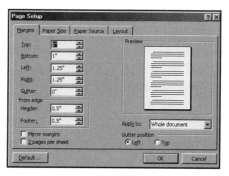

2. Type in or use the spin box controls to set the **Top, Bottom, Left,** and **Right** margins, and **Gutter** (left margin space for document binding).

3. Type in or use the spin box controls to set the size of the **Header** and **Footer** from the edge.

4. Click the **OK** [OK] button to accept changes and return to the document.

Change from Portrait to Landscape

1. Choose **File, Page Setup; Paper Size** tab.

2. Select the **Orientation** of **Portrait** (8.5 by 11 inches) or **Landscape** (11 by 8.5 inches). Click the **OK** [OK] button to accept changes and return to the document.

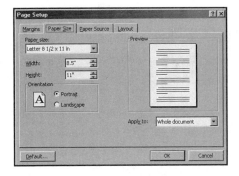

Select the Paper Size

1. Choose **File**, **Page Setup**; **Paper Size** tab.

2. Select the **Paper size** from the drop-down list box. The Width and Height options alter automatically, although you can alter them with the spin box controls.

3. Click the **OK** [OK] button to accept changes and return to the document.

Select the Paper Source

1. Choose **File**, **Page Setup**; **Paper Source** tab.

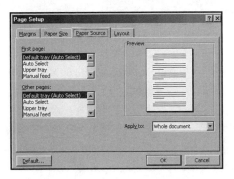

2. Select which printer tray you want the first page to come from. This is convenient if you want the first page of a document to have special paper, such as letterhead.

3. Select which printer tray you want the other pages to come from.

4. Click the **OK** [OK] button to accept changes and return to the document.

Alter the Document Layout

1. Choose **File, Page Setup; Layout** tab.

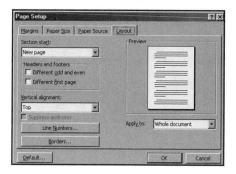

2. Select whether the **Headers and footers** are displayed as **Different odd and even** or **Different first page**.

3. Select from any of the other layout options and click the **OK** [OK] button to accept changes and return to the document.

See Also Alignment, Breaks, Columns, Print, Print Preview

PAGINATION

When you fill a page with text or graphics, Word inserts an automatic page break and starts a new page. You can prevent single lines from appearing by themselves at the top or bottom of a page with pagination controls.

Apply Pagination Control

1. Select the paragraph for which you want to control the pagination.

2. Choose **Format, Paragraph; Line and Page Breaks** tab.

3. Select from the following options:

   ■ **Widow/Orphan control**—Prevents the last line of a paragraph from printing by itself at the top of a page or the first line of a paragraph from printing by itself at the bottom of a page.

   ■ **Keep lines together**—Prevents a page break within a paragraph.

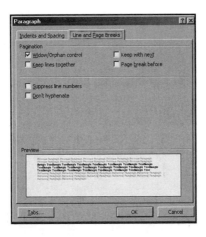

- **Keep with next**—Prevents a page break between the selected paragraph and the following paragraph.

- **Page break before**—Inserts a manual page break before the selected paragraph.

- **Suppress line numbers**—Keeps line numbers from displaying next to selected paragraphs.

- **Don't hyphenate**—Excludes a particular paragraph from hyphenating automatically.

4. Click the **OK** button to accept the changes and return to the document.

See Also Breaks, Page Setup, Tabs

PARAGRAPH SPACING

Word allows you to set the amount of vertical space between all paragraphs or two specific paragraphs.

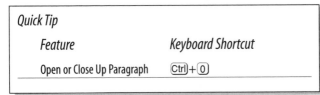

Quick Tip	
Feature	*Keyboard Shortcut*
Open or Close Up Paragraph	Ctrl + 0

P
Q
R

Alter Paragraph Spacing

1. Select the text for which you want to alter the spacing. Or, click somewhere in the paragraph.
2. Choose **Format, Paragraph; Indents and Spacing** tab.
3. Click the **Spacing Before** and **After** spin boxes and select the point size you want.
4. Click the **OK** ⬚ button to accept changes and return to the workbook.

See Also Character Spacing, Fonts, Line Spacing, Text

PASTE

You can share information within and between documents in Word (and other Windows applications) by pasting text and objects. You can now paste up to 12 different items from the Clipboard at a time. The Clipboard is where items are stored after you copy or cut them.

Quick Tips		
Feature	*Button*	*Keyboard Shortcut*
Paste	🗐	Ctrl+V or ⬆Shift+Insert
Paste Format		Ctrl+⬆Shift+V

Paste Text or Objects

1. Place the cursor in the location where you want to place the text or object. You must have already cut or copied text or an object in order for the **Paste** 🗐 button to be active.
2. Click the **Paste** 🗐 button on the Standard toolbar.

Paste Multiple Items

1. Choose **View, Toolbars, Clipboard** to open the Clipboard toolbar. You must have already cut or copied text or an object for there to be any items on the Clipboard.

2. Place the cursor in the location where you want to insert a cut or copied item.

Copy an item to the Clipboard. Paste all items in the document.

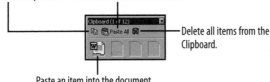

Delete all items from the Clipboard.

Paste an item into the document.

3. Move the mouse pointer over the items on the Clipboard toolbar and a ScreenTip displays what is contained in each clip (unless the clip is extensive, and then only part of it displays).

4. Move the mouse pointer to where you want to insert the text or object. Click the clip that you want to paste. When finished, click the **Close** ☒ button to close the Clipboard toolbar.

Paste Special

1. Place the cursor in the location where you want to place the text or object. You must have already cut or copied text or an object.

2. Choose **Edit, Paste Special** to open the Paste Special dialog box.

3. Click the **Paste** option to simply paste the item; click **Paste link** to create a shortcut link to the source file (any changes you make to the source file are reflected in your document). The **Paste link** option won't be available if your copied selection isn't linkable (for example, a piece of clip art you copied from the Insert ClipArt dialog box).

4. Select the **As** option for how you want to paste the item. The **Result** area of the dialog box explains each type of paste.

P

5. Click the **OK** button to accept changes and return to the document.

See Also Copy and Cut, Hyperlinks, Links, Move Text, Replace Text

PLACES BAR
see Save Documents   pg 128

PORTRAIT
see Page Setup   pg 112

PRINT

Word makes it easy to print a document and enables you to select the printer and document settings.

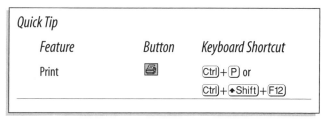

Quick Tip		
Feature	*Button*	*Keyboard Shortcut*
Print	🖨	Ctrl+P or Ctrl+⬆Shift+F12

Print Current Document Defaults

1. Click the **Print** 🖨 button on the Standard toolbar; the document prints according to the settings in your page setup.

Choose a Different Printer

1. Choose **File**, **Print** to open the Print dialog box.
2. Click the **Name** drop-down list box and select the printer you want to print to.

Enter Print Options

1. Choose **File**, **Print** to open the Print dialog box.

Prints the page where your cursor is currently located

Prints all pages in the document

Prints only the text that you selected before you opened the Print dialog box

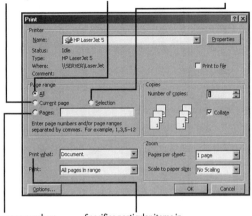

Prints any page numbers and/or page range you list

Specifies particular items in your document to be printed

2. Select the **Page range** that you want as your print job.

3. Select the **Number of copies** you want printed, and whether you want Word to **Collate** a multiple-page document.

4. Click the **Options** Options... button to select various printing options.

5. Click the **OK** OK button to accept any changes made and return to the main Print dialog box.

6. Click the **OK** OK button to send the print job to the printer.

P Q R

TIP

After you have started to print, the printing icon in the status bar displays the number of pages as it sends them to the printer. Double-clicking this icon while it is still sending to the printer immediately cancels the print job.

See Also Page Setup, Print Preview

P 120

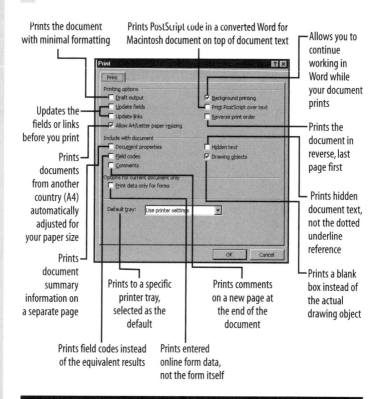

Prints the document with minimal formatting
Prints PostScript code in a converted Word for Macintosh document on top of document text
Allows you to continue working in Word while your document prints
Updates the fields or links before you print
Prints documents from another country (A4) automatically adjusted for your paper size
Prints document summary information on a separate page
Prints field codes instead of the equivalent results
Prints entered online form data, not the form itself
Prints to a specific printer tray, selected as the default
Prints comments on a new page at the end of the document
Prints the document in reverse, last page first
Prints hidden document text, not the dotted underline reference
Prints a blank box instead of the actual drawing object

PRINT PREVIEW

Print Preview enables you to see document pages onscreen as they will appear printed on paper, displaying page numbers, headers, footers, fonts, font sizes and styles, orientation, and margins.

Quick Tip

Feature	Button	Keyboard Shortcut
Print Preview	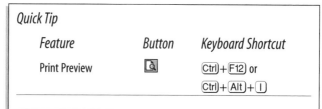	Ctrl+F12 or Ctrl+Alt+I

Preview a Document

1. Click the **Print Preview** button on the Standard toolbar.

2. Click the **Multiple Pages** 🔡 button on the Print Preview toolbar and click the number of pages you want to view at a time.

3. Click the **One Page** 🔲 button on the Print Preview toolbar to return to viewing one page.

4. Click directly on the previewed document and the magnification increases.

5. Click directly on the previewed document again and the magnification returns to the original percentage.

6. Click the **Close** Close button on the Print Preview toolbar to return to the document.

Edit in Print Preview

1. Click to deselect the **Magnifier** 🔍 button on the Print Preview toolbar.

2. Click anywhere in the previewed document and type your edits.

3. Click to select the **Magnifier** 🔍 button again when finished making your edits.

TIP

In addition to making edits in Print Preview, you can adjust margins and indents. Click to deselect the **Magnifier** 🔍 button on the Print Preview toolbar. If the ruler isn't displayed, click the **View Ruler** 🔲 button. Move the mouse pointer over the right or left margin lines on the horizontal ruler and click and drag the vertical dotted line that appears (do the same for the top and bottom margin lines on the vertical ruler). Select the text where you want to alter the indent. Click directly on the **Left Indent**, **Right Indent**, **Hanging Indent**, or **First Line Indent** markers and drag them to the desired location on the ruler.

P
Q
R

See Also Page Setup, Print, Views, Workspace

PRINT LAYOUT VIEW

see Views   pg 168

PROPERTIES

Details about a file that help identify it—author's name, document title, topic, keywords—are known as file properties. Use file properties to help organize your files or display file information. This can be convenient information to have saved if you need to search for a particular file.

Add Document Summary Information

1. Choose **File**, **Properties**; **Summary** tab.

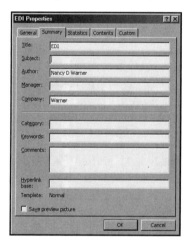

2. Type the information about your document that you want to save.

3. Click the **OK** button to return to the document.

Read Document Statistics

1. Choose **File**, **Properties**; **Statistics** tab.

2. Review the statistical information about your document.

3. Click the **OK** button to return to the document.

See Also Files

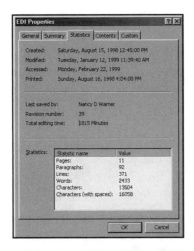

PROTECT DOCUMENTS

You can restrict the types of changes users make to a document by adding document protection. In addition, you can assign a password to prevent unauthorized users from editing or unprotecting the document.

Protect a Document

1. Choose **Tools, Protect Document** to open the Protect Document dialog box.

2. Select the options from **Protect document for**.

Highlights all reviewer changes to track them

Does not let a reviewer change document content, but does let him insert comments

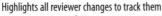
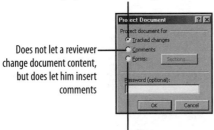

Protects a document from changes except in form fields or unprotected sections

> **TIP**
>
> You can apply protection to particular sections in your docu-
> ment, as long as you have inserted section breaks. Choose the
> **Protect document for Forms** option, click the **Sections**
> `Sections...` button to specify the particular section in the
> Section Protection dialog box, and click the **OK** `OK` button
> to return to the Protect Document dialog box.

3. Type and reenter any passwords that need to be con-
firmed when Word provides a Confirm Password dialog
box, and then click the **OK** `OK` button.

4. Click the **OK** `OK` button in the Protect Document
dialog box to accept changes and return to the document.

> **CAUTION**
>
> Don't forget the password you assign to your documents. If you
> forget or misplace the password, you will not be able to access
> the document again. Choose a password you can remember but
> that others can't guess. Avoid names of pets or family. The hard-
> est passwords to guess are at least five characters long and con-
> tain at least one symbol character, such as $, %, &, or @.

See Also Comments, Share Documents, Track Changes

QUIT
see Exit Word   pg 52

REDO
see Undo and Redo   pg 165

REPLACE TEXT

In Word, you can replace text, character and paragraph formatting, and special characters.

Quick Tip

Feature	*Keyboard Shortcut*
Replace	Ctrl+H

Search and Replace Text

1. Choose **Edit**, **Replace** to open the Find and Replace dialog box.

2. Type the text you want to change in the **Find what** text box. Any text from a previous search will still be in the dialog box, unless you have exited Word.

3. Click in the **Replace with** text box (or press the Tab⇄ key) and type the text you want to replace it with.

4. Select from the Search and Replace options.

Replace the first occurrence that satisfies the criterion and immediately move to the next occurrence, if there is one.

Search for the next occurrence that satisfies the criterion.

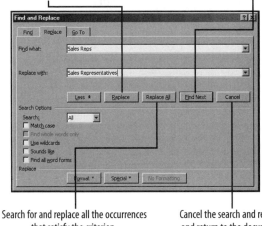

Search for and replace all the occurrences that satisfy the criterion.

Cancel the search and replace and return to the document.

5. Click the **OK** ⬛ OK button when Word tells you how many replacements were made. If there is no text that satisfies the criteria, Word alerts you with a message box that no changes have been made.

Perform an Advanced Replace

1. Choose **Edit**, **Replace** to open the Find and Replace dialog box.

2. Click the **More** ⬛ More ⫶ button to expand the **Search Options** in the dialog box.

3. Type the text you want to change in the **Find what** text box and enter your new text in the **Replace with** text box. Any text from a previous search will still be in the dialog box; unless you have exited Word.

4. Select from the various **Search Options** for the find and replace items:

   - **Match case**—For example, instead of finding all occurrences of lowercased *sales*, you can search specifically for initial capped *Sales*.

   - **Find whole words only**—For example, this will find *the* instead of also finding *them* and *they* (this is inactive if there are multiple words).

   - **Use wildcards**—For example, this will find character occurrences using the following *wildcards*: ? * [ ]. *R?t* will find *rot* and *rat*; *r*t* will find *replenishment* and *rut*; *r[ao]t* will find *rot*, *rat*, and *root*.

   - **Sounds like**—For example, this will find phonetically similar text such as *too*, *to*, and *two*.

   - **Find all word forms**—For example, this will find different word forms like *eat*, *ate*, and *eaten*.

5. Click the **Format** [Format ▾] button to select a particular format; click the **Special** [Special ▾] button to select particular characters for the find and replace items; click the **No Formatting** [No Formatting] button to remove any applied formats.

6. Select from the find and replace buttons.

7. Click the **OK** [OK] button when Word tells you how many replacements were made. If there is no text that satisfies the criteria, Word alerts you with a message box.

8. Click the **Cancel** [Cancel] button to exit the Find and Replace dialog box.

TIP

In addition to replacing text, you can search and replace on formatting options only, which is considered a no text format. Simply enter a format into the **Find with** and the **Replace with** boxes using the **Format** `Format ▾` button to select the particular formats.

See Also Browse, Copy and Cut, Find Text, Format Painter, Go To, Paste, Undo and Redo

RIGHT MOUSE BUTTON

When you right-click an item in your workspace, a shortcut menu appears (also known as a pop-up or context menu). Shortcut menus include the commands you use most for whatever is currently selected.

Use a Shortcut Menu

1. Right-click an object or some text.

2. Click a command on the shortcut menu that appears; the menu automatically goes away and the command is performed.

TIP

To leave a shortcut menu without making a selection, press the Esc key or click elsewhere on the desktop.

See Also Menus

RULERS
see Indents   pg 79

P
Q
R

SAVE DOCUMENTS

Save the document you are working in to store it for later retrieval. A good practice is to save your documents frequently as you work in them.

Quick Tips

Feature	Button	Keyboard Shortcut
Save	🖫	Ctrl + S or
		Shift + F12 or
		Alt + Shift + F2
Save As		F12

Save a Document

1. Click the **Save** 🖫 button on the Standard toolbar to save any recent changes. If you haven't saved the document yet, the Save As dialog box appears.

Most recent 80 files   Places bar   Files in the My Documents folder (sometimes called the Personal folder)

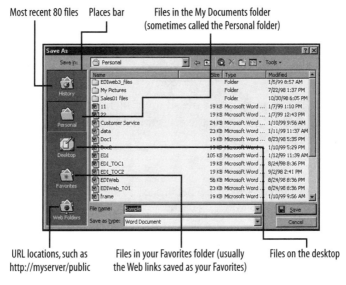

URL locations, such as   Files in your Favorites folder (usually   Files on the desktop
http://myserver/public   the Web links saved as your Favorites)

2. Click the **Places bar** option for the location of the file you want to save.

3. Click the **Save in** drop-down list box to help locate the correct folder or drive. You can also click the **Up One Folder** button to move through folders.

4. Type the **File name** and click the **Save** button.

Save as a Different Name

1. Choose **File, Save As** to open the Save As dialog box.
2. Click the **Places bar** option for the location of the file you want to save.
3. Click the **Save in** drop-down list box to help locate the correct folder or drive. You can also click the **Up One Folder** button to move through folders.
4. Type the new **File name** and click the **Save** button.

Save as a Different File Type

1. Choose **File, Save As** to open the Save As dialog box.
2. Click the **Places bar** option for the location of the file you want to save.
3. Click the **Save in** drop-down list box to help locate the correct folder or drive. You can also click the **Up One Folder** button to move through folders.
4. Click the **Save as type** drop-down list box and select the desired file type.
5. Type the **File name** and click the **Save** button.

See Also Close, Open Document, Versions, Web Pages

SCREENTIPS
see Toolbars   pg 161

SEARCH
see Find Text   pg 55

SECTIONS
see Breaks   pg 18

SHADING

You can apply colors and shades to the background of selected text. You can also follow the same steps to change the text shade to something different.

Shade Text

1. Select the text that you want to shade.

2. Choose **Format, Borders and Shading; Shading** tab.

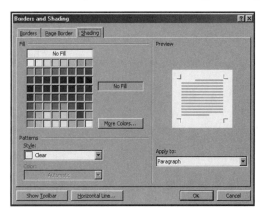

3. Select a color in the **Fill** area and click the **Style** drop-down list box to apply a pattern to the background of the text. You can also click the **Color** drop-down list to select the pattern.

4. Click the **OK** button to accept changes and return to the document.

TIP

Keep in mind that colors print as shades of gray unless you use a color printer; so don't use too dark a color if you are printing to a non-color printer.

See Also Borders, Fonts

SHARE DOCUMENTS

You can share documents either by restricting access to the document or by preventing changes from being made within each particular document.

Set File Share Options

1. Choose **Tools, Options; Save** tab.
2. Select the **File sharing options for** your document.

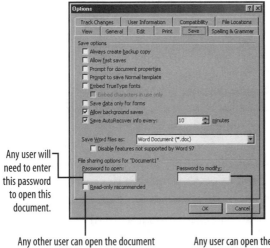

Any user will need to enter this password to open this document.

Any other user can open the document but changes made must be saved with a different filename.

Any user can open the document but will need to enter this password to make any edits.

3. Type your password; when Word prompts you with a Confirm Password dialog box, reenter your password and click the **OK** [ok] button.
4. Click the **OK** [ok] button in the Options dialog box to accept changes and return to the document.

See Also Comments, Track Changes

SPACING
see Paragraph Spacing   pg 115

SPECIAL EFFECTS
see Text Effects   pg 158

S
T
U

SPELLING AND GRAMMAR

Word 2000 shows red wavy lines under any misspelled words and green wavy lines under any sentences that are grammatically problematic.

Quick Tips

Feature	Button	Keyboard Shortcut
Spelling and Grammar	ABC✓	F7
Next Misspelling		Alt+F7

Check Spelling and Grammar

1. Click the **Spelling and Grammar** ABC✓ button on the Standard toolbar. The Spelling and Grammar dialog box opens, displaying the first spelling or grammar error it finds.

2. Click the appropriate spelling option in the **Suggestions** list box; if one doesn't work, type the change directly in the **Not in Dictionary** list box.

3. Click the appropriate button to make the selected **Suggestions** change.

TIP

The **Options** Options... button opens the Spelling and Grammar dialog box, which allows you to change the Word rules for checking spelling and grammar as well as open a different custom dictionary.

---

4. Click the **Yes** Yes or **No** No button if Word asks you to continue checking the document; for example, if you didn't start checking at the beginning of the document.

5. Click the **OK** OK button if Word displays a message telling you the spelling and grammar check is complete. This means all inaccuracies have been reviewed.

In-Text Correction

1. Right-click any words with red wavy lines and select the suggested spelling correction from the shortcut menu.

2. Right-click any words with green wavy lines and select the suggested grammar correction from the shortcut menu.

See Also AutoCorrect, Thesaurus

SPLIT WINDOW

You can simultaneously view two parts of document if you split the window into two panes. This is convenient when you need to view information at the beginning of a document, in order to work in another portion of the document.

Quick Tips	
Feature	*Keyboard Shortcut*
Close Split Pane	Alt + ⬆Shift + C
Split Document	Alt + Ctrl + S
Other Pane	F6 or ⬆Shift + F6

Split the Document View

1. Choose **Window**, **Split** and click in the document where you want to view the split area. You can click and drag the split bar at any time to adjust the size of each window.

2. Move through each split with the scrollbars to position the document view areas.

3. Double-click the split bar to return to viewing just one part of the document; or choose **Window**, **Remove Split**.

See Also View Multiple Documents, Views, Workspace

S
T
U

START WORD

When Word is installed, a copy of the application icon is placed in the Programs menu by default. From this menu, you can launch Word.

Use the Start Button

1. Click the **Start** `▓Start` button in the taskbar to open the Start menu.
2. Click the **Programs** command to open the Programs menu.
3. Click **Microsoft Word** to start the application.

Create and Use a Shortcut Icon

1. Locate the Word folder or file (even Word's executable file .exe) in Windows Explorer.
2. Left-click the folder or file and drag and drop it at the new location, such as your desktop.
3. Select **Create Shortcut(s) Here** from the pop-up menu that appears; the shortcut is created.
4. Double-click the shortcut icon to launch Word.

See Also Exit Word, Switch Between Documents and Applications

STYLES

Word 2000 has numerous format styles for you to choose from when formatting text. Instead of applying a particular format to text, you can apply a style that formats the text the same way each time.

Quick Tips

Feature	*Keyboard Shortcut*
Style	`Ctrl`+`⬆Shift`+`S`
Normal Style	`Ctrl`+`⬆Shift`+`N`
Reset Characters	`Ctrl`+`Spacebar` or `Ctrl`+`⬆Shift`+`Z`
Reset Paragraph	`Ctrl`+`Q`
Apply Heading 1	`Ctrl`+`Alt`+`1`
Apply Heading 2	`Ctrl`+`Alt`+`2`
Apply Heading 3	`Ctrl`+`Alt`+`3`

Apply a Word Style

1. Select the text you want to style.
2. Click the **Style** drop-down list to select the style you want to apply.

Create a New Style

1. Select the text you want to format as a style. Then, format the text the way you want it to appear both in this file as well as in similar documents in the future.
2. Type the new name in the **Style** drop-down list box area and press the `⏎Enter` key.
3. Click the **Style** drop-down arrow to see your new style listed.

Modify a Style

1. Choose **Format**, **Style** to open the Style dialog box.

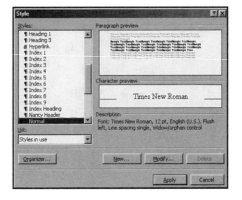

2. Click the **Modify** [Modify...] button to open the
   Modify Style dialog box and review the style
   Description.

3. Click the **Format** [Format ▾] button and modify the style
   as necessary.

4. Click the **OK** [OK] button when finished formatting
   the style.

5. Click the **Apply** [Apply] button to return to the document; any text in your document with the modified
   style is updated.

S
T
U

> **TIP**
>
> The next time you exit Word, you will be notified that you made a change to your global Word template and asked if you want to save the changes. If you want to keep the new or modified style, click the **Yes** [Yes] button; otherwise click the **No** [No] button.

Delete a Style

1. Choose **Format**, **Style** to open the Style dialog box.

2. Click the style you want to delete from the **Styles** list box.

3. Click the **Delete** [Delete...] button and you will be asked whether you want to delete the styles. Click the **Yes** [Yes] button to delete the style; click the **No** [No] button to return to the Style dialog box.

4. Click the **Apply** [Apply] button to return to the document; any text in your document with the deleted style will become the Normal style.

Copy Styles

1. Open the document that you want to apply styles from your Normal.dot global template. The document you open will be the current document.

2. Choose **Format**, **Style** to open the Style dialog box.

3. Click the **Organizer** [Organizer...] button to open the Organizer dialog box, which should default to the **Styles** tab. The right side **Styles available in** drop-down list box should be set to the template you want to copy styles from (for example, the Normal.dot global template); the left side **Styles available in** drop-down list box should be set to the current document you opened. If either are incorrect, select the drop-down list boxes and select the appropriate documents.

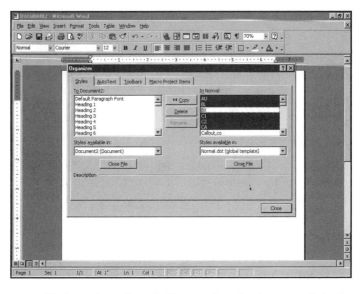

4. Click in the right side **To template** list box area (which should be Normal.dot) and select one or all of the styles you want to copy to your current document (press the Ctrl key while selecting noncontiguous styles in the list; press the ◆Shift key while selecting contiguous styles in the list).

TIP

Keep in mind that if you copy all the styles from a template, you may as well load the template in your document. See the section on Templates for more information.

---

5. Click the **Copy** ◀◀ Copy button to copy the styles from the Normal template to apply them to your document.

6. Click the **Close** Close button when finished copying the styles.

TIP

You can also copy styles from a document to your Normal.dot global template. Simply click to select the styles on the left side **In *document*** area and copy them to the right side **To *template*** area.

See Also Fonts, New Document, Templates, Text

SUMMARY
AutoSummarize   pg 10

SWITCH BETWEEN DOCUMENTS AND APPLICATIONS

You can have multiple Office applications and Word documents open at a time and switch between them whenever you want. You can use the Windows taskbar to move quickly from one open application window or Office document to another.

Quick Tip

Feature	*Keyboard Shortcut*
Switch Between Open Documents and Applications	Alt + Tab

Switch Between Documents and Applications

1. Click the taskbar button for the document you want to use.
2. Click the taskbar button for a different Office application.

See Also Start Word

SYMBOLS

The Symbol command enables you to insert symbols, special characters, and international characters.

Quick Tips

Feature	*Keyboard Shortcut*
Symbol Font	Ctrl + Shift + Q
Em Dash	Alt + Ctrl + - (numeric keyboard)
En Dash	Ctrl + - (numeric keyboard)
Nonbreaking Hyphen	Ctrl + ⎵
Optional Hyphen	Ctrl + -
Nonbreaking Space	Ctrl + Shift + Spacebar
Copyright	Alt + Ctrl + C
Registered	Alt + Ctrl + R
Trademark	Alt + Ctrl + T
Ellipsis	Alt + Ctrl + .
Single Opening Quote	Ctrl + `, `
Single Closing Quote	Ctrl + ', '
Double Opening Quote	Ctrl + `, "
Double Closing Quote	Ctrl + ', "

Insert a Symbol

1. Click the cursor in the text where you want to add the symbol.

2. Choose **Insert, Symbol**; **Symbols** tab. You can locate different symbols and different types of symbols by clicking the **Font** drop-down arrow and selecting from the different fonts. Each font provides you with a different symbol selection.

3. Double-click the symbol you want to insert into your document.

4. Click the **Close** ☒ button to return to the document.

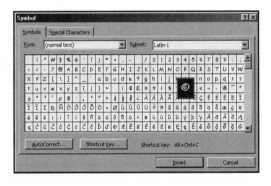

Insert Special Characters

1. Click the cursor in the text where you want to add the symbol.

2. Choose **Insert, Symbol**; **Special Characters** tab.

3. Double-click the **Character** you want to insert into your document.

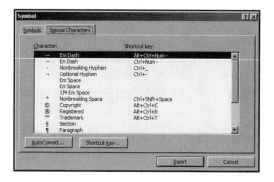

4. Click the **Close** ⊠ button to return to the document.

Delete a Symbol

1. Select the symbol in the text.
2. Press the Del key.

Insert a Foreign Letter

1. Click the cursor in the text where you want to add the symbol.
2. Choose **Insert, Symbol**; **Fonts** tab.
3. Click **(normal text)** from the **Font** drop-down list box. Click the appropriate **Subset** language.
4. Double-click the **Foreign Letter** you want to insert into your document.
5. Click the **Close** ⊠ button to return to the document.

See Also AutoCorrect, Fonts

TABLES

Instead of creating long lists of information and trying to cross-reference these lists, you can simply add a table to your document.

Quick Tips

Feature	*Keyboard Shortcut*
End of Column	Alt + PgDn
End of Row	Alt + End
Column Break	Ctrl + ↑Shift + ↵Enter
Next Cell	Tab↹
Previous Cell	↑Shift + Tab↹
Start of Column	Alt + PgUp
Start of Row	Alt + Home

Draw Table

1. Click the **Tables and Borders** button on the Standard toolbar; the pointer becomes a pencil and the Tables and Borders toolbar appears.

2. Click in the document and drag to draw the outer border of the table.

3. Click inside the table and draw the rows and columns.

S
T
U

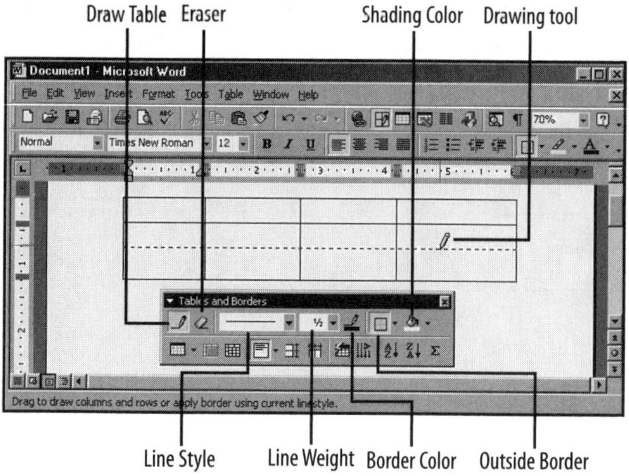
Draw Table
Eraser
Shading Color
Drawing tool
Document1 - Microsoft Word
Tables and Borders
Drag to draw columns and rows or apply border using current linestyle.
Line Style
Line Weight
Border Color
Outside Border

4. Click the **Draw Table** button on the Tables and Borders toolbar to deselect the drawing feature, which converts the pointer back to a cursor so that you can add data to the table.
5. Click the **Close** button to close the Tables and Borders toolbar, or choose **View**, **Toolbars**, **Tables and Borders** to toggle the toolbar closed.

Insert Table

1. Click the **Insert Table** button on the Standard toolbar and select the number of rows and columns you want from the drop-down box.
2. Click the cursor in the table cells and type to add the data.

> **TIP**
>
> To save time, set your page margins before you insert a table. Otherwise, you have to select all the tables and alter the margins afterwards—which can be tricky.

Alter Table Text Wrapping and Alignment

1. Click in the table that you want to position in your document.
2. Choose **Table, Table Properties**; **Table** tab.

3. Select the **Text wrapping** option (for example, **Around** wraps document text around the table).

4. Select the **Alignment** option of **Left**, **Center**, or **Right**. You can also choose the **Indent from left** spin box to increase or decrease the indent.

5. Click the **OK** ⟨ OK ⟩ button to accept changes and return to the tdocument.

Work with Columns

1. Move the mouse pointer over the right edge of the column you want to alter. When the mouse pointer changes to a two-headed arrow, click and drag the column to the new size.

2. Click the top border of a column (when the pointer becomes a black down arrow) to select it.

3. Right-click and choose **Insert Columns** from the shortcut menu to add a column to the left of the selected column.

4. Right-click the column again and choose **Distribute Columns Evenly** from the shortcut menu to make each column the same size.

5. Right-click the column again and choose **Delete Columns** from the shortcut menu; that column is deleted.

Work with Rows

1. Move the mouse pointer over the bottom edge of the row you want to alter. When the mouse pointer changes to a two-headed arrow, click and drag the row to the new size.

2. Click the left border of a row (when the pointer becomes a white right arrow) to select it.

3. Right-click and choose **Insert Rows** from the shortcut menu to add a row above the selected row.

4. Right-click the row again and choose **Distribute Rows Evenly** from the shortcut menu to make each row the same size.

5. Right-click the row again and choose **Delete Rows** from the shortcut menu; that row is deleted.

AutoFormat Table

1. Click in any cell of the table you want to format.

2. Choose **Table, Table AutoFormat** to open the Table AutoFormat dialog box.

3. Click an option in the **Formats** list to view a preset format sample in the **Preview** area. If you want, you can choose from the **Formats to apply** and **Apply special formats to** sections to modify the AutoFormat before you apply it.

4. Click the **OK** button to accept changes and return to the document.

Alter Cell Alignment

1. Right-click a cell and choose **Cell Alignment** from the shortcut menu; click the alignment style from the submenu.

Merge Table Cells

1. Select the cells that you want to merge together.

2. Choose **Table**, **Merge Cells** to combine the information in the cells.

Split Table Cells

1. Select the cells that you want to split.

2. Choose **Table**, **Split Cells** to open the Split Cells dialog box.

3. Click the **Number of columns** and **Number of rows** spin boxes so that they display the number of columns and rows that you want the cell to become.

4. Click the **OK** button to separate the information in the cells.

Split a Table

1. Click the cursor in what will be the first row of the new table.

2. Choose **Table**, **Split Table** to create two separate tables.

Repeat Header Rows

1. Select the row that you want to be a repeat header on multiple pages.

2. Choose **Table**, **Heading Rows Repeat**. Select this command again if you want to alter or stop the repeating row header.

Apply Formulas

1. Click the cursor in the cell where you want to enter a formula.

2. Choose **Table**, **Formula** to open the Formula dialog box with Word's best guess at the formula you want (usually SUM). If there is a blank cell, you need to place a 0 in it to perform the calculation properly.

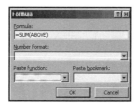

3. Click the **Paste function** drop-down list box if you want a different function. Make sure that there is an equal ⊟ sign before the function you select and that the cells you want calculated are listed in the brackets ⬅ ⬅. Cells are A1, B1, A2, B2, and so on, just like in a worksheet.

4. Click the **Number format** drop-down list box if you want a different number format applied to the contents of the cell.

5. Click the **OK** button to accept any formula changes and return to the document.

Format Text Direction

1. Select the cells that you want to alter the text direction.

2. Choose **Format, Text Direction** to open the Text Direction - Table Cell dialog box.

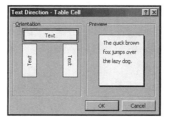

3. Click the desired **Orientation**.

4. Click the **OK** button to accept changes and return to the document.

Convert Table to Text

1. Select the table you want to convert.

2. Choose **Table, Convert, Table to Text** to open the Convert Table to Text dialog box.

3. Select the desired **Separate text with** option and click the **OK** [OK] button; the table is now Normal styled text.

Convert Text to a Table

1. Select the text you want to convert.

2. Choose **Table, Convert, Text to Table** to open the Convert Text to Table dialog box.

3. Select the **Number of columns** for the **Table size**, the desired **Separate text at** option, and then click the **OK** [OK] button; the text is now a table.

AutoFit Table Data

1. Select the table cells you want to AutoFit.

2. Choose **Table, AutoFit** and select from the available options:

   - **AutoFit to Contents**—adjusts the table column width depending on the amount of text.

   - **AutoFit to Window**—automatically resizes the table when displayed in a Web browser window.

   - **Fixed Column Width**—current column widths become fixed widths.

150

- **Distribute Rows Evenly**—selected rows become equal in height.
- **Distribute Columns Evenly**—selected columns become equal in width.

Sort Table Data

1. Select the table you want to sort.
2. Choose **Table**, **Sort** to open the Sort dialog box.

3. Click the **Sort by** drop-down list box to determine the initial sort (two more additional sorts can be assigned in the **Then by** drop-down list boxes).
4. Click the **Type** drop-down list box to choose between a **Text**, **Number**, or **Date** sort. Then, choose the **Ascending** or **Descending** sort option.
5. Click the **OK** button to accept changes and see how the sort affects the table.

See Also AutoFit, AutoFormat, Borders, Columns

TABLE OF CONTENTS

A table of contents can be used to organize and navigate your document. Click any page number in the table of contents and you immediately move to the corresponding document heading.

Quick Tip	
Feature	*Keyboard Shortcut*
Mark Table of Contents Entry	Alt + ⬆Shift + O

Create a Table of Contents

1. Apply Word built-in heading and outline styles—or your own custom styles—throughout the document.

2. Choose **Insert, Index and Tables; Table of Contents** tab.

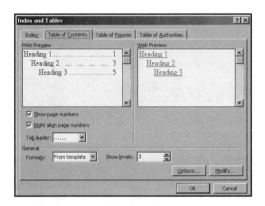

3. Click the **Options** button if you want the table of contents to be built with styles in addition to the default Heading 1, Heading 2, and Heading **3.**

4. Click through the **Available styles** and type in the desired numeric **TOC level**.

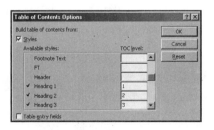

5. Click the **OK** button when you have finished selecting the styles.

6. Click the **OK** button to select the default preview options, and the table of contents is built and displayed at the location of your cursor.

See Also AutoSummarize, Index, Outline, Styles

152

TABS

You can align tabs in different positions in your documents to indent text. In addition, you can assign multiple tab stops and select leader type tabs or clear your tabs at any time.

Set a Tab

1. Click in the paragraph where you want to set a tab (usually at the beginning, but not always).

2. Click the Tab and Indent Setting at the left end of the horizontal ruler to toggle through and choose the type of tab.

Tab and Indent Setting: Click to toggle through tabs and indent options.　　Decimal Tab: Align a decimal point at the tab stop; extends text or numbers without a decimal point to the left of the tab stop.　　Right Tab: Extend the text to the left from the tab stop.

Left Tab: Extend the text to the right from the tab stop.　　Center Tab: Center the text at the tab stop.　　Bar Tab: Insert a vertical line at the tab stop.

3. Move the mouse pointer to the place on the ruler where you want the tab stop, and click once.

4. Press the (Tab⇆) key to align the text with the tab stop.

Delete Tabs

1. Click in the paragraph or select the text in which you want to delete a tab stop.

2. Click the tab stop on the ruler and drag it off the ruler. This will only remove the tab from the currently selected text, not the entire document.

TIP

You can move a tab stop by clicking the tab indicator on the ruler and dragging it to the desired location on the ruler.

S
T
U

Set Tab Stops

1. Choose **Format, Tabs** to open the Tabs dialog box.

2. Click the type of tab you want to set in the **Alignment** area (**Left, Center, Right, Decimal,** or **Bar**).

3. Click whether you want to apply a **Leader** tab (none, dotted line, dashed line, or solid line).

4. Type a measurement for the **Tab stop position** and click the **Set** [Set] button.

Clear Tab Stops

1. Choose **Format, Tabs** to open the Tabs dialog box.

2. Click the **Tab stop position** and click the **Clear** [Clear] button; or click the **Clear All** [Clear All] button to remove all the tab stops.

See Also Alignment, Character Spacing, Indents, Page Setup

TEMPLATES

You can create a document template with any type of text, formatting, toolbars, macros, styles, and just about any other setting you can change.

Create and Open a New Document Template

1. Click the **Open** button on the Standard toolbar to open a new document. Type in the text and format it how you want the document template to appear.

2. Click the **Save** button on the Standard toolbar to open the Save As dialog box.

3. Click the **Save as type** drop-down list box and select **Document Template**. Any newly created document templates automatically default to the **Templates** folder and have a **.dot** file extension.

4. Type a **File name** and click the **Save** button. You can make modifications to this document template at any time—just make sure you save the changes.

S
T
U

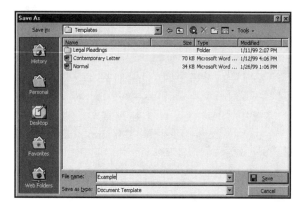

5. Choose **File, Close** to close the document.

6. Choose **File, New; General** tab.

7. Click the document template you just created and saved.

8. Click the **Create New** option of **Document**.

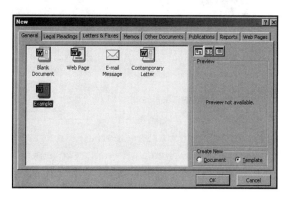

9. Click the **OK** [OK] button to open the template as a document.

Attach a Document Template

1. Open the document you want to attach a document template to.

2. Choose **Tools, Templates and Add-Ins** to open the Tools and Add-ins dialog box.

3. Click the **Attach** button and double-click the document template **File name** from the Attach Template dialog box. This is the default document template location. If the template you want to attach is not in this folder, either move the file before continuing or locate the file and continue.

4. Click the **Automatically update document styles** option so that any styles in the document template update the styles in your current document. Click the **OK** button.

See Also Add-Ins, New Document, Save Documents, Styles

TEXT

To draw attention to important text in a document, you can make the text any combination of bold, italic, and underlined.

Quick Tips

Feature	Button	Keyboard Shortcut
Bold	**B**	Ctrl+B
Italic	*I*	Ctrl+I
Underline	U	Ctrl+U
Double Underline		Ctrl+Shift+D
Word Underline		Ctrl+Shift+W

Set Text Options Before Typing

1. Click the **Bold** ![B], **Italic** ![I], and/or **Underline** ![U] buttons before you begin typing.

2. Type text into your document and it will be formatted as you type.

Bold Text

1. Select the text you want to format bold.

2. Click the **Bold** ![B] button on the Formatting toolbar; click the **Bold** ![B] button again to remove the bold.

Italicize Text

1. Select the text you want to format with italics.

2. Click the **Italic** ![I] button on the Formatting toolbar; click the **Italic** ![I] button again to remove the italics.

Underline Text

1. Select the text you want to format underlined.

2. Click the **Underline** ![U] button on the Formatting toolbar; click the **Underline** ![U] button again to remove the underline.

See Also Alignment, Case Change, Character Spacing, Fonts, Text Box, Text Effects

TEXT BOX

A text box is a drawing tool that creates a container for text in your document that you can resize and move like a graphic.

Add a Text Box

1. Click the **Drawing** ![icon] button to open the Drawing toolbar.

2. Click the **Text Box** ![icon] button on the Drawing toolbar or choose **Insert, Textbox**.

3. Click in the document and drag the cross-hatch pointer to the desired shape size.

4. Type the information you want in the text box.

Format a Text Box

1. Click in the text box to select it.

2. Choose **Format, Text Box** to open the Format Text Box dialog box.

3. Select from the various tabs to format the text box:

   ■ **Colors and Lines**—Change the color that fills in the text box and display particular types of lines around the text box.

   ■ **Size**—Size and rotate the text box as well as alter the scale.

   ■ **Layout**—Alter the wrapping style of the text box (how text is flowed around or over the object) and the alignment of the text box in the document.

   ■ **Text Box**—Adjust the internal margins of the text box. You can also convert the text box to a frame.

   ■ **Web**—Type the text you want to display while a Web browser is loading the text box.

4. Click the **OK** [OK] button on any of the tabs to accept changes and return to the document.

Link Text Boxes

1. Insert text boxes throughout your document that you want to link. Do NOT type any text into the text boxes before you link them.

2. Right-click on the first text box to link and choose **Create Text Box Link** from the shortcut menu. The pointer becomes a cup with an arrow; move the pointer to the next text box to link to and click in the text box when it appears to be pouring the contents. Repeat this process for each text box you want the link to continue to.

3. Choose **View, Toolbars, Text Box** to open the Text Box toolbar.

4. Click in the first linked text box.

S
T
U

5. Type the text that you want in the linked text boxes. Any text that doesn't fit in the first text box will flow over to the next linked text box.

Create Text Box Link   Previous Text Box   Change Text Direction

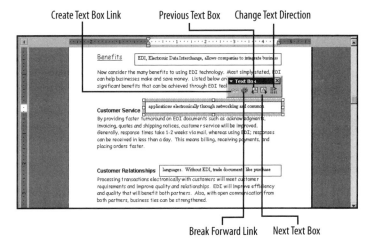

Break Forward Link   Next Text Box

6. Click the **Close** ☒ button to close the Text Box toolbar and return to working in the document.

See Also Drawing Tools, Forms, WordArt

TEXT EFFECTS

Word lets you add animated effects to text so that it appears to move or flash in documents that will only be viewed or read online.

Create Text Animation

1. Select the text that you want to animate.
2. Choose **Format**, **Font**; **Text Effects** tab.
3. Click the **Animations** you want to apply and view them in the Preview area.
4. Click the **OK** [OK] button to accept changes and return to the document.

Remove Text Animation

1. Select the text that you want to stop animating.

2. Choose **Format, Font; Text Effects** tab.

3. Click the **Animations** option of **(none)**.

4. Click the **OK** ![OK] button to accept changes and return to the document.

See Also Fonts, Text

THEMES

Instead of or in addition to adding background color, you can apply a document theme. A theme is a set of related design elements and color schemes for background images, bullets, fonts, and other document elements. This helps create consistent-looking documents and Web pages.

Apply a Document Theme

1. Click in the document (or particular frame) where you want to apply a theme.

2. Choose **Format, Theme** to open the Theme dialog box.

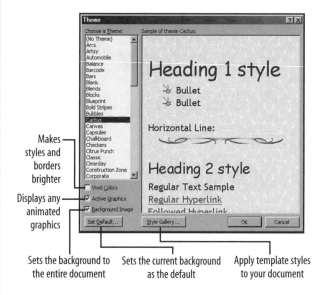

Makes styles and borders brighter

Displays any animated graphics

Sets the background to the entire document

Sets the current background as the default

Apply template styles to your document

3. Click a preset theme in the **Choose a Theme** list box. Click the **OK** button and apply the theme to your document.

TIP

You can apply a different theme to different frames in your Web document. Keep in mind that this might not be the most visually appealing option, but you can practice applying themes this way.

See Also Background, Frames, Views, Web Pages

THESAURUS

Word's Thesaurus is a convenient tool that helps you replace words with a synonym, antonym, or related word.

Quick Tip	
Feature	*Keyboard Shortcut*
Thesaurus	(Shift)+(F7)

Use the Thesaurus

1. Choose **Tools, Language, Thesaurus** to look up the word nearest the cursor in the Thesaurus dialog box.

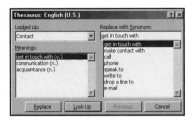

2. Click the synonym you like for the word in the **Replace with Synonym** list box.
3. Click the **Look Up** button to look up another word in the **Meanings** list.
4. Click the **Replace** button to insert the new word; the Thesaurus dialog box then disappears.

See Also Spelling and Grammar

TOOLBARS

To perform tasks and access features quickly and easily, you can click a toolbar button with your mouse pointer. Doing so is faster than using a menu command, especially for frequent or repetitive tasks. The Standard toolbar contains buttons for the most common commands. The Formatting toolbar contains lists and buttons for the most common formatting commands.

Float and Dock a Toolbar

1. Click the vertical bar on the leftmost side of the toolbar, and drag and drop the toolbar onto your desktop so that it looks like it is floating on top of your desktop.
2. Click the toolbar title and drag it to a different edge on the desktop so that it looks like it is docked.
3. Double-click the title portion of the toolbar and the toolbar automatically returns to its previous location.

S
T
U

Show and Hide Toolbars

1. Choose **View, Toolbars,** and select the toolbar you want to show. Toolbars that are displayed have a check next to their name in the menu.

2. Choose **View, Toolbars,** and deselect the toolbar you want to hide. The check in the menu and the toolbar onscreen disappear.

Add or Remove Buttons

1. Click the **More Buttons** ⬛ button on the toolbar you want to customize and select **Add or Remove Buttons.**

2. Check a particular command button to add it to the toolbar; uncheck a command button to remove it from the toolbar.

Create a New Toolbar

1. Choose **Tools, Customize; Toolbar** tab.

2. Click the **New** ⬛ New... ⬛ button, type in the name of the new toolbar, and click the **OK** ⬛ OK ⬛ button.

3. Click the **Commands** tab in the Customize dialog box and select a button from the **Categories** and **Commands** list boxes.

4. Click and drag the command to the location you want and drop it on a toolbar.

5. Click the **Close** ⬛ Close ⬛ button on the Customize dialog box.

Modify a New Toolbar Command Button Image

1. Choose **Tools, Customize; Commands** tab.
2. Select the toolbar category.
3. Click the command button on the toolbar you want to modify; it appears with a black line around it.
4. Choose **Modify Selection, Change Button Image**, and select an image.
5. Click the **Modify Selection** [Modify Selection ▼] button and choose **Default Style**, which displays only the button image.
6. Click the **Close** [Close] button on the Customize dialog box.

See Also Menus

TRACK CHANGES

Sometimes you find that you have to make corrections in a document, or perhaps you are working on a report in a team environment. To determine who made what changes when, you can track the changes onscreen with revision marks.

Quick Tip		
Feature	*Button*	*Keyboard Shortcut*
Track Changes		Ctrl+⬆Shift+E

Track Document Changes

1. Right-click the **Track Changes** TRK button on the status bar and choose **Track Changes** from the shortcut menu. The **TRK** will be grayed out before the Track Changes is activated.

2. Type some changes into the document. The new text appears as a different color and underlined. Any changes to a line are flagged by a vertical black bar in the margin.

Alter Viewable Changes

1. Choose **Tools, Track Changes, Highlight Changes** to open the Highlight Changes dialog box.

2. Select from the available tracking options.

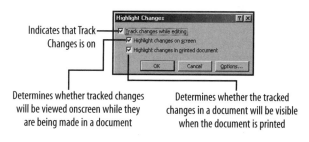

Indicates that Track Changes is on

Determines whether tracked changes will be viewed onscreen while they are being made in a document

Determines whether the tracked changes in a document will be visible when the document is printed

3. Click the **Options** Options... button to alter the Track Changes colors according to inserted text, deleted text, changed formatting, or changed lines. This is convenient when multiple people are editing a document; they can each be assigned a different color.

4. Click the **OK** OK button in both dialog boxes to accept changes and return to the document.

See Also Accept or Reject Changes, Comments, Protect Documents, Share Documents, Versions

TROUBLESHOOT
see Help   pg 72

TYPEFACE
see Fonts   pg 57

UNDERLINE
see Text   pg 155

UNDO AND REDO

Undo and Redo are convenient when you want to see how your document looks with and without changes you make. You can undo and redo text changes, formatting options, and more.

Quick Tips

Feature	Button	Keyboard Shortcut
Undo	↶	Ctrl+Z or Alt+←Backspace
Redo or Repeat	↷	Ctrl+Y or Alt+⇧Shift+←Backspace or F4 or Alt+↵Enter

Use Undo and Redo

1. Type or make change(s) in your document.
2. Click the **Undo** ↶ button as many times as necessary to undo the change(s).
3. Click the **Redo** ↷ button as many times as necessary to redo the change(s).

S
T
U

See Also Close, Save Documents

UPPERCASE

see Case Change   pg 21

VERSIONS

Word's versions feature allows you to save and manage multiple versions of a document in a single file. Then you can review, open, print, and delete earlier versions as necessary.

Save Document Versions

1. Choose **File, Versions** to open the Versions dialog box.

2. Click the **Automatically save a version on close** option if you want a different version to save each time you close the document.

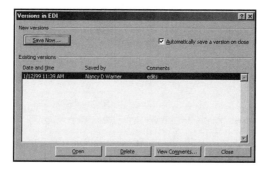

3. Click the **Save Now** [Save Now...] button to open the Save Version dialog box, type any notes in the **Comments on version** text box, and click the **OK** [OK] button. If you haven't saved the document yet, you are prompted with a Save As dialog box.

4. Type a **File name** and click the **Save** 🔲 Save button. If you have saved the document already, click the **Close** Close button to return to the document.

Review Existing Versions

1. Open the document that you have saved a document version of. Before you can modify an earlier version, you must open that version and use the Save As command to save it as a separate file.

2. Choose **File**, **Versions** to open the Versions dialog box.

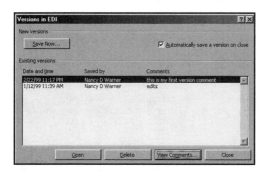

3. Click one of the **Existing versions** and click the **Open** Open button to view the document; click the **View Comments** View Comments... button to review your version notes; click the **Delete** Delete button to delete the version.

4. Click the **Close** Close button to return to the document.

> **TIP**
>
> You cannot modify a saved version of a document unless you open a particular version and save it with a different filename.

V
W
X

See Also Comments, Protect Documents, Save Documents, Share Documents, Track Changes

VIEW MULTIPLE DOCUMENTS

If you don't want to constantly switch between documents, you can view multiple Word documents onscreen. The document displaying a darker title bar is considered the active document; when you type, text appears there.

View Multiple Documents

1. Open all the documents you want to view simultaneously.
2. Choose **Window**, **Arrange All**. All open documents are automatically arranged next to each other.
3. Click on the title bar or in the body of the document you want to work in.

> **TIP**
> To return to viewing only one entire document, double-click the title bar of the document you want to work in.

See Also Open Document, Split Window, Workspace

VIEWS

Word provides many ways to view documents; each view has its purpose. You can quickly switch between each view and utilize the features available.

Quick Tips

Feature	Button	Keyboard Shortcut
Normal View		Ctrl+Alt+N
Web Layout View		Ctrl+Alt+W
Print Layout View		Ctrl+Alt+P
Outline View		Ctrl+Alt+O

Switch Document Views

1. Choose the view button to the left of the horizontal scrollbar according to the view you desire.

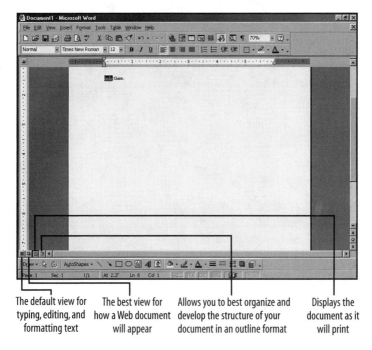

The default view for typing, editing, and formatting text	The best view for how a Web document will appear	Allows you to best organize and develop the structure of your document in an outline format	Displays the document as it will print

> **TIP**
>
> In addition to the shortcut keys and buttons, you can access the different views from the View menu.

See Also Document Map, Print Preview, Web Pages, Workspace

WATERMARKS

Images that appear grayed out behind text are called watermarks. An electronic watermark can be made by typing text over a graphic image.

Create a Watermark

1. Right-click a graphic that you have inserted or created in your document and choose **Format Picture** from the shortcut menu.

2. Click the **Color** drop-down list in the **Image control** section and choose **Watermark**.

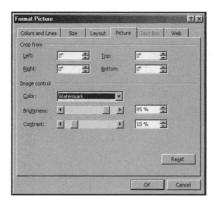

3. Click the **Layout** tab and select the **Behind text** option for the **Wrapping style**.
4. Click the **OK** [OK] button to accept the changes and return to your document.

See Also Clip Art, Print, Text Box

WEB LAYOUT VIEW
see Views   pg 168

WEB PAGES

You can view your documents as Web pages in Web Page Preview even before you have saved the file as a Web page. Once you save a document as a Web page, you can load it to your Web site. In addition, Word provides you a wizard and templates that will help you create your own Web pages.

Quick Tips		
Feature	*Button*	*Keyboard Shortcut*
Web Go Back	⬅	(Alt)+(⬅)
Web Go Forward	⮕	(Alt)+(➡)

Use Web Page Preview

1. Choose, **File**, **Web Page Preview** to open the Internet Explorer browser and display your document.

2. Click the **Back** ⬅ button to return to the Word document.

Save as a Web Page

1. Choose **File**, **Save as Web Page** to open the Save As dialog box.

2. Click the **Places bar** option for the location of the file you want to save.

3. Click the **Save in** drop-down list box to help locate the correct folder or drive. You can also click the **Up One Folder** 🔼 button to move through folders.

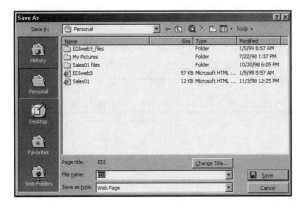

4. Click the **Change Title** [Change Title...] button and type in a **Page title** if you want the Web page title to be different than the filename, and click the **OK** [OK] button.

5. Type the **File name** and click the **Save** [Save] button.

Use the Web Page Wizard

1. Choose **File**, **New**, **Web Pages** tab to open the New dialog box Web page templates and wizard.

2. Double-click on the **Web Page Wizard** icon.

V
W
X

3. Click the **Next** <kbd>Next ></kbd> button to begin entering information into the wizard. Use the **Next** <kbd>Next ></kbd> and **Back** <kbd>< Back</kbd> buttons as you move through the wizard and the **Finish** <kbd>Finish</kbd> button when finished.

Use Web Page Templates

1. Choose **File, New, Web Pages** tab to open the New dialog box Web page templates and wizard.

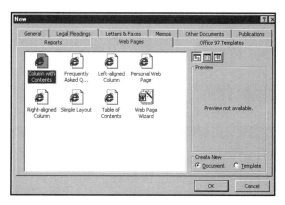

2. Double-click on the Web page template icon you want to create, edit the document as necessary, and save the document as a Web page.

See Also Background, Frames, Themes, Views

WILDCARD
see Replace Text   pg 124

WORDART

WordArt is a feature that allows you to insert text that looks graphical itself. You can select from different styles of colors and arrangements of lettering.

Add WordArt

1. Click the **Drawing** button on the Standard toolbar to open the Drawing toolbar.

2. Click the **WordArt** button on the Drawing toolbar.

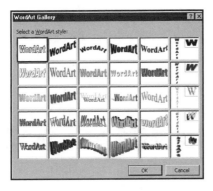

3. Double-click a WordArt style in the WordArt Gallery dialog box and type the text in the Edit WordArt Text dialog box.

4. Click the **OK** [OK] button to insert the WordArt and return to your document.

Edit WordArt

1. Double-click the WordArt object to edit the text, the font, and/or the font size; click the **OK** [OK] button to return to the document.

2. Click directly on the WordArt object and drag it to a new location, or click the mouse pointer on one of the object handles and drag to resize the WordArt.

See Also Clip Art, Drawing Tools, Files, Objects

WORD COUNT

Word provides statistics about your documents so you can track the number of pages, words, characters, paragraphs, and lines.

Find Word Count

1. Choose **Tools**, **Word Count** to open the Word Count dialog box.

2. Click the **Cancel** [Cancel] button when you finish reviewing the **Statistics**.

See Also AutoSummarize, Properties

WORKSPACE

You can click the scrollbars to move the view of the document; press the arrow keys on the keyboard to move the cursor through the document; use the zoom control to see various amounts of the document at once; or view/hide the rulers or review a document in full screen.

Quick Tips

Feature	Button	Keyboard Shortcut
Minimize Document Window	▣	
Maximize Document window	▣	Ctrl + F10
Move Document Window		Ctrl + F7
Restore Document Window	▣	Ctrl + F5
Size Document Window		Ctrl + F8

Use Scrollbar Options

1. Click the scrollbar arrows to scroll through the document. Or, click directly on the scrollbar itself and drag it up and down to quickly move through the document.

2. Click the **Previous Find/Go To** ⬆ and **Next Find/Go To** ⬇ buttons to move through the document by page.

3. Click the **Select Browse Object** ◉ button to browse through the document using different features: **Go To; Find; Browse by Edits, Heading, Graphic, Table, Field, Endnote, Footnote, Comment, Section,** or **Page.**

Increase Document View Size

1. Click the **Zoom** drop-down list on the Standard tool-bar.

2. Select the percentage or descriptive size you want to view your document in. You can also click directly on the **Zoom** list box and type in an exact zoom percentage.

View Rulers

1. Choose **View, Rulers** to toggle between the rulers being displayed or hidden.

View Full Screen

1. Choose **View, Full Screen** to view the document with only the Full Screen toolbar to close the full screen. You can move the mouse pointer to the top of the screen and the menu commands appear.

2. Press the Esc key or click the **Close Full Screen** Close Full Screen button to return to the previous view.

See Also Browse, Document Map, Views

ZOOM

see Workspace   pg 174

V
W
X

INDEX